Friday Night, Saturday Night

Youth Cultural Identification In The Post-Industrial City

Robert G. Hollands

Published by
The Department of Social Policy
Claremont Bridge Building
University of Newcastle
Newcastle Upon Tyne
NE1 7RU

ISBN 0 903891 01 8

Cover photo courtesy of The Journal

I would like to dedicate this book to two people who were tremendously influential in motivating me to pursue and indeed complete this research. First, to Jim Atkinson ('Uncle Jimmy' from Montreal), who first got me interested in drinking culture, and who surely must now be granted the honorary title of 'Professor of Alcohol Studies'. And to the memory of my other uncle, Richard Ingman (1946-1992)- wherever you are, I hope they have bar stools.

Wild Night

As you brush your shoes
And stand before the mirror
And you comb your hair
And you grab your coat and hat
And you walk wet streets
Tryin to remember
All the wild night breezes
In your mem'ry ever
And everything looks so complete
When you're walkin' out on the street
And the wind catches your feet
And sends you flyin', cryin'
Ooh-wee!
The wild night is calling, alright
And all the girls walk by
Dressed up for each other
And the boys do the boogie-woogie
On the corner of the street
And the people passin' by
Just stare in wild wonder
And the inside juke box
Roars out just like thunder
And everything looks so complete
When you're walkin' out on the street
And the wind catches your feet
And sends you flyin', cryin'
Ooh-wee!
The wild night is calling
The wild night is calling
The wild night is calling
Come on out and dance
Come on out and make romance

- words and music by Van Morrison (1987)

CONTENTS

Acknowledgements

During the course of this research I received an enormous amount of support and help from a wide variety of people and organisations. First and foremost I would like to especially thank all those young 'Geordies' and students who took part in the interviewing process. I hope I have managed to convey something of the 'lived experience' of going out and that the 'structure of feeling' (to quote the late Raymond Williams) associated with this activity has not been completely lost in its translation into print. I learnt a great deal from all of the respondents and made some good friends along the way.

Second, there are a number of individuals who assisted in this project in various ways. Rob MacDonald played a triple role as an academic colleague, friend and informed participant by offering help and advice throughout the research, as well as introducing me to a great group of Bigg Market 'lads'. A special thanks to Vernon Gayle who continued to embellish my reputation as 'Boozy Bob' even if it wasn't true. Helen Carr offered unending support, lived through the many indulgences academic research demands and also carried out one of the early pilot interviews. As the research assistant, Rosalind Taylor carried out all but three of the interviews with female respondents, wrote up fieldnotes and assisted in preparing the data for analysis. Thanks also to Mo O'Toole, Ann Maines, John Dunne, Carolyn Young, Sue Wilkinson, Alastair Bonnett, Robin Humphrey, Jane Wheelock, Pete McCarthy, Richard Bott, David Buck, Lindey Carr and Andy Balman. My Urban Sociology students provided a good forum for trying out new ideas and Wallsend Harriers provided light relief from work. I am also indebted to Les Gofton's previous work on drink and the city and Chief Inspector Pears of Northumbria Police was very helpful and furnished me with a range of useful material on crime and disorder in the city. Carol Hellier of Data Preparation Service was extremely patient and Sheila Carter was responsible for translating speech to text, complete with Geordie spelling! Justin O'Conner, Andy Lovatt, Derek Wynne and the whole 'Manchester School' from the Institute for Popular Culture at Manchester Metropolitan University provided encouragement as well as great company in Coimbra, Portugal, while Alan Sande of the Norland Research Institute in Bodo, offered some very useful comparative material on young people's use of alcohol in the ritual process in Norway. Last, but not least, thanks to the ESRC for providing initial funding for this project.

This book first appeared as 'Department of Social Policy Working Paper No. 2', University of Newcastle (March 1995). A special thanks to Chris Sullivan, managing director of Scottish and Newcastle Retail and John Goddard, Dean of Law, Environment & Social Sciences, University of Newcastle, for financial assistance in the publication of this research report into a book. It should be noted however, that the report was conducted prior to and independent of this support, and reflects the views of the author only.

Dr. Robert G. Hollands
Newcastle Upon Tyne
September 1995

List of Tables, Figures, Maps and Interviews

Tables

Figures

Maps

Transcribed Interviews

Summary

This book explores one important aspect of contemporary youth cultures- the phenomenon of 'going out'. The main argument is that the social significance and meaning of going out has been transformed from a simple 'rite of passage' to adulthood towards a more permanent 'socialising ritual' for young adults, and that this change is due to broader shifts in economic, domestic and cultural life.

Rapid economic and educational change, delayed transitions into marriage and separate households, declining communities, and the availability of new consumption lifestyles, have resulted in a prolonged or 'post-adolescent' phase whereby traditional adult roles cannot be so easily assumed or assimilated. This has had the effect of forcing some young adults to 'reinvent' themselves elsewhere, resulting in both a differentiation of youth cultures and styles and the (re)creation of local, social and personal identities in relation to the city. These different forms of social interaction expressed in the night time economy, including group drinking rituals, fashion, music, and dance and drug cultures are, in essence, modern equivalents of community.

Two of the fundamental processes underlying this shift of emphasis from 'rites to rituals' are: (1) economic restructuring and its effect on work, education and domestic identities and (2) the increasing role the city plays in shaping young adult's experiences of modern life. Rapid economic change has blocked young adult's opportunities to inherit previous occupational cultures, weakened community links and delayed transitions out of the family household. The shift from these more traditional sites of identities to increased identification with the city through consumption, and their participation in extended socialising rituals, represents a broader response and re-adjustment by young people to 'modernity' and post-industrialism.

The existence of these extended transitions and shifts in the sites whereby young people construct their identities, has had several significant and contradictory effects. One of the most important ones has been that involvement in youth cultures and nightlife rituals have simultaneously become a more central and stable aspect of identity formation, as well as creating a space for activities, attitudes and behaviours which are neither youthful nor adult. Evidence supporting this view is reflected in our findings concerning the frequency of nights out, the percentage of income spent on this activity and the various cultural forms through which young adults express themselves.

This shift of meaning and social context is exemplified in terms of some of the obvious changes in nightlife culture (city and peer group-based, more young women, an increase in provision for students and the proliferation of styles), but is also obscured somewhat by the continued use of traditional symbols like alcohol and assumptions that going out is still motivated primarily by courtship rituals. While these remain important aspects of the activity, our research shows that the confirmation of cultural identity and socialising with friends are increasingly becoming the primary reasons for having nights out.

Paradoxically, involvement in such cultures can both reflect and stand in for the loss of traditional identities, while also allowing young adults to step outside of established roles. A second effect then has been an increased fragmentation of youth identities and cultures in the contemporary period. Blocked or delayed transitions has meant that some young adults have sought to symbolically revive traditional local identities by playing out what it means to be a 'Geordie' on city centre streets and pubs, while others have struggled to move outside dominant social expectations and utilise this new found space to create alternative identities in relation to gender, sexual orientation, politics, student subcultures, not to mention a range of music, drug and dance based lifestyles.

Shifts in the meaning and social context of going out have also changed fundamentally because of the dramatic increase in the numbers of women in the city at night. Our research reveals that women go out more frequently, would feel worse if restricted, and spend a higher percentage of their income on nights out than their male counterparts. Despite the persistence of historical and contemporary barriers, they have made significant leaps forward in terms of reforming their own identities in relation to the city, and have played a central role in promoting the socialising aspect of going out. While young women continue to be influenced by domestic and sexual ideologies, female solidarity in dance and drug cultures and 'ladies only' nights out are examples of these changes.

Failure to recognise the effect of these broader transformations and the changed meaning and social context of going out has resulted in various misinterpretations about the phenomenon in question. For instance, there has been a tendency to substitute adult concerns, expressed much of the time as 'moral panics', in place of some of the desires, needs and problems faced by young people caught up in a rapidly changing life world. Much of the public discourse is either cloaked in assumptions about the historic function of nights out as a 'rite of passage', or is shrouded in a set of negative images revolving around violence, inebriation and promiscuity. This book calls into question many of these images and assumptions and argues for a more sensitive reinterpretation of young adult's behaviours and nightlife cultures. This is not to argue that there are no social problems concerning young people and the city or that various policy suggestions and experiments should not be proposed. Our respondents raised a whole series of important issues including division and conflict in the city (racism, homophobia and sexual harassment as well as violence), improvements in services, a general lack of investment in youth cultural activity, over-regulation in terms of policing and licensing, and a lack of imaginative and alternative night time provision. The policy relevance of the book is derived from the views and experiences of young adults themselves and is based not on a social control model imposed from above, but one designed to enhance cultural creativity and different social possibilities emanating from below.

'Extraordinary though it may seem, Tyneside is not now famous for its manufacturing industries, but for its shopping malls, nightclubs and flashy cocktail bars' (Robinson, 1988)

1. Introduction

This book explores one important aspect of contemporary youth cultures- the phenomenon of 'going out'. The main argument it makes is that consumption, particularly in the use and appropriation of evening city space, is becoming a more central element in the production of youth identities and that this is due primarily to fundamental changes in economic, domestic and cultural life. The combined effect of these broader social changes is significant in how we come to understand and respond to young adults' new identities, values and activities, as well as has important policy implications for how cities are shaped and used by their inhabitants.

The centrality of cities as a focus for youth cultures is at least well recognised if not well understand. Even a casual observer could not fail to notice a ritual descent of young adults onto city centre streets at least every Friday and Saturday night. City councils and universities have increasingly made reference to the quality of nightlife to attract students, businessmen and tourists, while social commentators, journalists and film-makers have written articles and made various documentaries/ films on young people's use and monopolisation of city centres. As Elms (1988) notes in the magazine **The Face**, 'there has been a general realisation that the culture of young Britain is now a nightclub culture'.

Despite a long history of social science writing on youth, particularly through the 1970s and 80s, the relationship between city space, culture and youth identity has remained relatively unexplored. The few academic sources there are have only begun to scratch the surface of this phenomenon or have chosen to explore specific aspects of this important social issue.[1] Unfortunately, this has meant that the public has had to rely on either media-inspired or 'official' accounts of young adults use of cities, which has often resulted in a 'social problem' or 'moral panic' approach to this topic.

Media approaches by their very nature focus on the extreme and the dramatic, while remaining highly critical of any alternative analysis of such a 'common sense' phenomenon. This perhaps explains journalist's continuing fascination with certain aspects of youth, yet apparent disdain of sociological analysis in this field. 'News values' tend to focus around negative aspects of youthfulness, like crime, deviance and disorder, rather than viewing and understanding young people's values and behaviours as either a positive metaphor for social change or as a response to wider societal issues. This is not to suggest young people do not experience problems, or sometimes form part of them, but rather to argue it is how we come to understand and interpret such situations that is crucial.

Sociological research on youth cultures then is often greeted with derisory comments from the media and this project proved no exception. Before it had even commenced, national media coverage of the research criticised it for being common sense and a waste of money, attracting such headlines as 'Boozy Bob's Going on a £16,000 Pub Crawl' (Daily Star, 28.8.93). Local newspapers and television also highlighted the cost and 'pedestrian' nature of the project, labelling it as the so called 'Bigg Market drinking study', rather than picking up on its wider concern with the changing meaning and social context of young adult's leisure practices, and their connection to a rapidly evolving economic, domestic and cultural landscape (see for example some of the emotive headlines in **Figure 1**)[2].

Of course media responses towards young people, and more specifically to youth cultures in the city, are closely tied to official reactions and proclamations from those powerful in society (i.e. 'primary definers' or 'moral entrepreneurs' to use some sociological phrases). While rural areas are not immune, it is the city, with its historical imagery of disorder, impersonality and crime, that gets public attention. From football hooliganism to lager louts, ravers, noisy students and squatters, the urban backdrop is very much in view. Other issues such as poverty and homelessness often get second billing while some of the more positive images surrounding youth cultures- the vast amounts of time, energy and money put into fashion, music, art, dance and consumption in cities- get even less coverage.

Local politicians are located in an ambivalent if not contradictory position in this regard. On the one hand, they are left with the often difficult task of image-building their city and ensuring local economic development. Clearly, a vibrant nightlife enhances business and youth cultures can play a valuable role in this process. On the other hand, local politics is often overshadowed by national policy and dominant interests and the youth issue can easily slip between a 'lassie-faire' approach and social problem perspective. Interestingly enough, local

10   DAILY STAR, Saturday, August 28 1993

BOOZY BOB'S GOING ON £16,000 PUB CRAWL

▶ £16,000 study of night life rapped as absurd waste

A BIGG MISTAKE!

By PETER YOUNG
Municipal Editor

★   TODAY Saturday August 28 1993   19

£16,000 grant..to go on pub crawl

by MARTIN EMMERSON

LECTURER Bob Hollands has been given a £16,000 grant to study boozing for a year.

He broke no academic bravely agreed to take on the task of discovering what makes bars tick

Bob to study wine, song and women

£16,000 to study city's wine bars

By PHILIP DERBYSHIRE

A UNIVERSITY lecturer is to be paid £16,000 to study . . . wine bars.

Social sciences expert Dr Bob Hollands will visit some of the nation's rowdiest watering holes, watching customers' behaviour.

Over the next year he will join revellers at Newcastle's Bigg Market, which has a reputation for drink-fuelled violence.

He will be funded by the Economic and Social Research Council.

The Newcastle University lecturer says his study will help people to understand wine bar culture.

He said: "Some people think all I'm interested in is looking at women and having a good time, but that isn't the case.

"Popular culture is a complex subject and needs to be studied properly."

But the scheme was condemned by city council Liberal Democrat leader John Shipley.

He said: "It is absurd and frivolous to waste public money on such a scheme. I would do it myself for the price of a pint.

"Anybody with a modicum of common sense knows what the Bigg Market is all about."

Dr Hollands has already begun recruiting would-be drinking companions to study.

He wants to study their behaviour to see if there are unwritten rules for having a good night out.

Sipping wine in the name of research

By Colin Wright

ARMED with a £16,000 grant from the Government-funded Economic and Social Research Council, Dr Robert Hollands is poised to undertake the gruelling year-long task of sipping the odd drink and watching the world go by as part of important research into the social phenomenon of youth and the wine bar.

Lunchtimes and evenings will be dedicated to keeping a clear head while observing the complex interaction of young men and women enjoying themselves over a bottle or two.

Dr Hollands, a lecturer in social sciences at Newcastle University, will concentrate his study on the bustling Bigg Market area of the city.

The 37-year-old Canadian plans to conduct detailed interviews with around 20 people aged between 18 and 28 and shadow them in their leisure time in an attempt to understand more about the present youth culture and the lure of the wine bar.

He explained yesterday: "The academic side is looking very much at how young people are constructing new identities in the leisure sphere.

"Obviously, this will entail shadowing people to wine bars, observing them and the bars of the Bigg Market to gain a better understanding.

"It is a misconception though to think I will be spending all my time drinking in bars. Most of the research will be conducted during interviews in the

homes of subjects where I will ask a range of questions in the context of their economic, educational and domestic situations."

Dr Hollands, who has a Phd in youth studies, said the project would be "hard work" and would be conducted mainly in spare time while he continued lectures at the university.

The grant, he insisted, would be used to pay for a part-time research assistant and the cost of transcribing taped interviews.

"I will produce a report on the life of the Bigg Market which people will find very useful," he said. "There is a lot of useful research never undertaken in this country because people are scared off by public opinion. That isn't going to happen to me."

The argument did not convince Mr John Shipley, Liberal Democrat leader of Newcastle City Council. He said: "It is absurd and frivolous to waste public money on such a scheme. I would do it myself for the price of a pint."

"Anyone with a modicum of common sense knows what the Bigg Market is all about and it doesn't need a costly research programme to tell us the obvious."

The Economic and Social Research Council, which has an annual budget of £50 million, said the project was "reasonable research" which would increase understanding about the social behaviour of young people.

DAILY MIRROR Saturday August 28 1993

£16,000 nights out are on us!

SCIENTIST Robert Hollands is getting a £16,000 Government grant to spend on nights out on the town.

The 37-year-old is to spend a year studying the nightlife in the boozy Bigg Market, Newcastle upon Tyne, one of the North's hottest spots.

Dr Hollands, a social sciences lecturer at Newcastle University, said he would not be slaughtering public cash on wild nights of wine, women and song.

And he vowed that he would pay for his own drinks and entertainment during the year long project out of his own pocket.

6

political response to this project ranged between these two poles. The ruling Labour group expressed mild curiosity, with the former Leader arguing that there was little they would expect to learn from the research. The Liberal Democrat councillor offered up his own analysis by equating youth cultures with drinking, demonstrating his lack of familiarity with both the research proposal not to mention the youth literature. Finally, the Conservative leader, not surprisingly, held up the 'law and order' banner by suggesting that the money for the research could have been utilised to buy another surveillance camera to more effectively control young adults in the city (Evening Chronicle, 27.8.93).

Rather than assume an implicit social problem perspective, the primary rationale of this research is to start with what young adults actually do on their nights out and seeks to provide them with a voice to interpret their own activities. Our data has been systematically collected and analyzed (see section two) and draws upon a cumulative total of approximately 270 years experience of going out and over 22,000 visits to the city centre by the young adults interviewed. As such, this book seeks to provide some basic information on patterns and elements of going out, many of which challenge official accounts and conventional wisdom on this issue (see section four).

Second, the book seeks to explain the growing importance and changing significance of the phenomenon of going out by looking at young people's wider social situation, including their economic, domestic and cultural background (see particularly section three). While we do not completely discount aspects of common sense about why young adults go out, the research is much more concerned with the wider socio-cultural meaning and context of youth cultures. Why, for example, are tribal customs in the Brazilian rainforest involving drug-taking, dancing, music and mating rituals, a legitimate and significant topic of inquiry for the anthropologist, while similar activities in western societies are seemingly inconsequential? Our research suggests that the growing importance of going out is directly linked to fundamental cultural and economic changes, which in turn have important implications for future local/ community, social and personal identities (see sections three, four and five). We would argue that such rituals are highly significant in that they both reveal wider social issues and concerns, as well as contain glimpses of important underlying social changes.

And so thirdly, the book offers up numerous policy suggestions of both a general and specific nature. Our view is that urban policy is often made either by those social group who have little or no experience of the phenomenon under question, or is devised in light of problematic official or media-based accounts. In terms of specific policy issues, we asked young adults a range of questions concerning city nightlife and how it could be improved, adapted and extended (see section six). In the conclusion, we argue for a more general policy shift regarding young people and the city, based not on a social control model imposed from above but one designed to enhance cultural creativity and different social possibilities emanating from below.

Finally, it is important to say a few words about specificity and generality in relation to the location of the research. It was conducted entirely in the city of Newcastle Upon Tyne and we make no apologies for confining the study to one such locality. All empirical work is bounded in space, place and time and recent discussions in the field of urban sociology appear to suggest some merit in studying the distinctiveness of cities, city space and local cultures within the broader context of global change (Savage and Warde, 1993). Newcastle is a vibrant, colourful city with a distinctive occupational history, accent, local tradition and spacial organisation. All of these aspects have hopefully been preserved in this book.

At the same time, Newcastle as a city also shares a number of characteristics with Britain's major industrial areas undergoing rapid economic change, with a dominant service economy, a major retail and leisure-based city centre, two universities and a thriving nightlife. While this research remains acutely aware of local effects and responses, it is undoubtably clear that young people all over the country, and indeed in the western world, are being exposed to similar experiences with respect to economic restructuring, changing family and household relations, urban regeneration and the globalisation of culture. In fact, it is the relationship between the general and the specific, the old and the new, and the local and the global, that lies at the heart of this analysis. Studying youth cultures in the city of Newcastle is, we would argue, highly illuminating in this regard.

The specificity of an event, a situation or a location cannot be grasped abstractly, which is why ethnographic methods proved so essential to understanding modern experience as it transpired in everyday life in the metropolis (Savage and Warde, 1993).

2. Methods and Sampling

The specific aim of the research was to explore and document the range of cultural meanings young adults attach to their evening use of urban space. The topic, by its very nature, necessitated the use of an interview-based, participant observation methodology- sometimes referred to as ethnography (see Hammersley, 1992). Appropriate sampling techniques however were adopted to maximise the representativeness and probability of the quantitative data collected (Bryman and Cramer, 1994). Following a pilot interview phase, the researchers utilised a combination of both random and quota sampling. Random samples of non-local students from both Northumbria and Newcastle University were obtained through appropriate personnel. Additionally, a random sample of local individuals, representing three different socio-economic wards, were contacted by post code addresses obtained from City Council records. Quota sampling was also used to supplement and broaden the local sample by matching our group of respondents with the known general characteristics of this age group made available in the 1991 Census for Tyne and Wear[3].

The key research instrument utilised was a semi-structured interview questionnaire designed to collect both quantitative and qualitative data, with emphasis on the latter. Information on social background factors, types and patterns of evening city centre use, the cultural meaning of going out and policy oriented questions were asked. Sixty young adults, between the ages of 16-31, were individually interviewed either in their homes or at the university, with sessions lasting from 45 minutes up to two hours. Interviews were taped and transcribed, with over 1500 pages of interview material being produced. The two main sub-groups included 30 locals (or 'Geordies') and 30 students from the two universities. The overall sample was 50% men and 50% female (interviewed by the principal researcher and female research assistant respectively). The principal researcher carried out additional group interviews and obtained shorter written questionnaires from 24

Newcastle University students for comparative purposes. A number of informal interviews were also carried out with student entertainment officers, police and security personnel, pub managers, bouncers, taxi drivers, DJs and bar staff.

No adequate ethnographic account can proceed solely on the basis of interviews with respondents. The researchers also made use of participant observation methods, accompanying a selected number of individuals on nights out. Twenty separate field visits were made over the course of the year, with approximately 60 pubs, clubs and music venues being visited. Some respondents were re-interviewed in light of the field visits, and much of this qualitative material forms the basis of the case studies reported in section five.

Youth remains a major symbolic investment for society as a whole (McRobbie, 1993)

3. Theorising Youth Identities in the Post-Industrial City

The main argument made in this book is that the social significance and meaning of going out has been transformed from a simple 'rite of passage' to adulthood, towards a more permanent 'socialising ritual' for young adults, and that this change is due to broader shifts in economic and cultural life. These changes have also been crucial in explaining paradigm shifts in the study of young people. There has been literally a pendulum swing in youth studies from an earlier concern with colourful and flamboyant working class subcultures of the 60s and 70s (like teds, mods, punks and skinheads, i.e. see Hall and Jefferson, 1976; Hebdige, 1979), to a somewhat bleaker analysis of the black and white iconography characterising research into youth unemployment, training and careers in the labour market in the 1980s (Banks et al, 1992; also see Griffin, 1993). Towards the end of the 80s both the public and social scientists appeared to be caught out by the emergence of new cultural forms like the so called 'acid house' and later 'rave' phenomenon. The revival of dance and drug based cultures, 'new ageism' and evidence of an increase in all types of youth cultural identification (West, 1993) came as somewhat of a surprise in the context of a continuing economic recession.

In theoretical terms, the difficulty has been to bridge the study of youth cultures and leisure with transitional studies emphasising the continuing role of work, education and the family, without compounding the inherent weaknesses of both perspectives. One approach attempting this emphasised the notion of 'broken transitions' and youthfulness as a 'new social state' (Willis, 1984), while other perspectives sought to renew a cultural analysis of young people within the rise of State policies in education and training (Hollands, 1990). More recently, a number of researchers have sought to recast the analysis of youth culture under a more 'post-modernist' banner (Redhead, 1993; McRobbie, 1993). We want to suggest that it is possible to begin to bridge this gap, without necessarily falling into the post-modernist maelstrom (MacDonald, 1994). In this study we argue

11

two of the fundamental processes underlying changes in contemporary youth cultures and the phenomenon of going out, are economic restructuring and the increasing role the city plays in shaping young adult's experience of modern life.

No analysis would be complete without investigating the impact economic change has had on young adults identities and transitions. Paramount to this restructuring process is the decline in manufacturing and shift towards service-based employment, changing production regimes organised around the concept of 'flexibility', an increase in women workers, and the global/spacial reorganisation of capital (Harvey, 1989; Bagguley, 1990). **Economic restructuring** is absolutely crucial in coming to terms with young people's opportunities and orientations towards work, the impact of unemployment on household organisation and the development of regional inequality, not to mentions its influence on changing patterns of consumption and the creation of a variety of different lifestyles.

A second process, which ironically has gone hand in hand with restructuring, concerns the increasingly important role cities play in relation to economic change, cultural consumption and the experience of **modernity** (Giddens, 1990). Modernity refers to our contemporary experience of the social world as one akin to being on a merry-go-round, intensely pleasurable at times, but often moving too fast leaving one to wonder where to get off. The city often reflects this mixed feeling of wonder and joy, anonymity and freedom on the one hand, and danger, vice and disorder on the other. Paradoxically, the city is also home to both the expression of regional identities and feelings of security and belonging, as well as increasingly becoming the primary site of the consumption of more global images, not to mention various 'risk' cultures central to many aspects of youthfulness (Beck, 1992).

The economic and industrial history of Tyneside is critical for a full understanding of young adults' cultures with respect to going out in the city. Sixty years ago the backbone of the North East economy was coal, shipbuilding and heavy industry and as late as 1971 manufacturing and work in the primary industries still accounted for 40% of employment in the area (Robinson, 1988). A strong patriarchal and masculine occupational identity (one of the original meanings of the term 'Geordie' is pit man or miner) spilled over into the wider local culture influencing the structure of home life, leisure and community.

The Tyneside economy of the 1990s is almost unrecognisable in light of this earlier history. The decline and collapse of employment in the primary industries is best represented by the closure of Ellington, the last pit in the North East, and the shipbuilder Swan Hunter being taken into receivership. Only 17% of local people now work in manufacturing, while over 70% are employed in the service sector, with many of these new jobs being part-time and filled by women (Tyneside Tec, 1992-3). Women's employment has risen over the last decade and they make up nearly half of the labour force, while male jobs have declined more dramatically, resulting in higher than average unemployment rates on Tyneside in comparison to both regional and national levels (Robinson, 1994).

The impact of these economic changes on young adults' identities and transitions is complex. Clearly one result concerns opportunities for employment. Census figures for Newcastle in 1991 show that just over half of 16-29 year olds are in either full or part time work with an employee, nearly 15% are classed as unemployed and just over 16% are students (this data and a comparison with our sample can be found in **Table One**).

The true extent of unemployment amongst this group is masked partly by 16-17 years olds' ineligibility to claim income support as well as a significantly high percentage of young women being classed as 'other inactive'. In short, young adults' economic prospects will have an important bearing on their attitudes and orientations to work and education, levels of income and spending, and living arrangements and transitions out of the family household. Furthermore, all of these factors impact upon both the patterns of and opportunities for going out.

While many young adults feel lucky to have a job at all, our research reveals that the move towards a so called 'post-industrial' service economy has not provided young adults on Tyneside with either a sufficiently strong work identity to replace that offered by the traditional occupational culture, nor enough money to enable them to set up households separate from their own families. Taking into account the different economic position of respondents in our sample (see **Table One**), the average net weekly amount of money local young men had was £102 (£144 for those in employment), while young women had £70 per week (£105 for those in employment).

Despite the fact that there have been some increased employment opportunities for young women in Newcastle,[4] which may have resulted in higher levels of sociability and self-esteem, many females are still limited to work in a narrow range of part-time, low paid servicing jobs, characterised by poor promotion prospects, a lack of training and low status. This paradox is represented well in the following

13

TABLE ONE

ECONOMIC POSITION OF YOUNG ADULTS
(16-29) IN NEWCASTLE

	All		Males		Females	
	(sample)	(Cen)	(sample)	(Cen)	(sample)	(Cen)
Employed (total)	56.7	51.0	60.0	51.9	53.4	50.1
(Full-time)	40.0	43.5	53.3	48.4	26.7	38.8
(Part-time)	16.7	7.5	6.7	3.5	26.7	11.3
Self-employed	-	2.6	-	3.8	-	1.3
Scheme	-	3.3	-	4.2	-	2.3
Unemployed	18.3	14.7	20.0	20.0	13.3	9.7
Eco Active	74.7	71.6	80.0	80.0	67.7	63.4
Student	23.3	16.4	20.0	17.6	26.7	15.2
Sick/retired and other inactive	2.0	12.0	-	2.3	6.6	21.4
Eco Inactive	25.3	28.4	20.0	20.0	33.3	36.6

(Source: 1991 Census for Tyne and Wear)

statement from one of our respondents[5] who worked in a travel agency:

Sue (L19) *Em, I love working with the public, because we're in reception, it's alright being under pressure cos everybody helps together, all the girls, it's really good fun. Just basically all the holidays, it's good working with it, it's exciting you know, booking people on holidays. I would like to be doing the same job, but more em, responsibility, you know, be taking over some part of the holidays rather than being an assistant. There is only one manager, whereas you could have like a supervisor, or something, moving up like you say.*

Young men's occupational choices and possibilities, while not quite so narrow, are also hampered by higher overall unemployment levels not to mention a dramatic decline in traditional forms of manual labour. Over half of the males in employment stated that they would prefer to be doing a different job in five years time. When asked whether they liked their current work, this was one typical response:

Doug (L31)   *No. The main reason, boredom, just boredom. There is no variation, no variation in the work. It is a typical desk job. The kind of work, dealing with child benefit, is not really something that holds a great deal of interest for me.*

Interestingly enough, while there was some indication that a section of young men continued to prefer manual work (Hollands, 1994), most of our sample, including women, expressed a strong desire for challenging professional careers.

The impact of economic change on young adult's job prospects, orientations and incomes has also had a significant 'knock on' effect on their opportunities to move out of the family household. Only 13% of our local sample lived on their own and only one of these individuals actually owned their flat. Fifty percent lived with their parent(s), while the remaining 37% either shared with friends or partners. Amongst men in particular, there was a distinct pattern of continuing to live at home well into the late 20's and even early 30s.

Marriage rates amongst young adults on Tyneside also support this pattern of delayed transitions into separate households due to economic circumstances (see **Table Two**). While fluctuations in marriage rates also reflect changing values in society, not to mention failing to capture an increase in cohabitation, the rate of decline almost perfectly parallels the dwindling job prospects for young adults in the area. According to Census figures from the last 30 years, it can be seen that marriage rates for all ages groups (between 15-29) have fallen by almost 50%, with the largest percentage drop amongst the 20-24 year olds (from 42.2% being married in 1961 compared to only 12.9% in 1991). Recently, there has been academic research suggesting that there has been a decline in moral respectability for the institution of marriage and fatherhood, particularly amongst young Northern working class men (Dennis and Erdos, 1992). Our research however revealed a relatively high regard amongst young men for their future responsibilities regarding partners and children even

TABLE TWO

MARRIAGE RATES (%) BY AGE AND SEX IN NEWCASTLE

	All Persons (ages)			Males (ages)			Females (ages)		
	(15-19)	(20-24)	(25-29)	(15-19)	(20-24)	(25-29)	(15-19)	(20-24)	(25-29)
1961	3.0	42.2	75.0	0.1	30.0	68.0	5.0	54.0	82.0
1971	4.8	40.0	71.3	2.4	31.4	65.0	7.3	50.0	78.0
1981	2.6	31.0	63.6	1.3	23.0	58.0	4.0	38.0	69.0
1991	0.9	12.9	42.4	0.4	9.0	37.0	1.4	17.0	47.0

(Source: Census)

though this commitment was most likely to revolve around traditional notions of being the 'breadwinner' and 'protector'. The vast majority of local men spoke about future relationships primarily in financial terms- for example, not being able to afford them.

Delayed transitions into marriage and autonomous households is the main coping mechanism young adults on Tyneside have in dealing with a less than satisfactory financial position. On the whole, the parental household appeared to be exceedingly generous in accommodating young family members, despite them sometimes being an increased monetary and domestic burden (Allatt and Yeandle, 1992). Young men in particular, while more able to contribute financially to the household income, did little domestic work with 67% of those living at home saying that the majority of the housework was done by someone else (usually mothers). There was however some evidence of changing household responsibilities, with a minority of sons and some fathers, particularly those who were long-term unemployed, sharing in the domestic duties (see also Wheelock, 1990). Young women tended to either share in or do the majority of domestic tasks regardless of the type of household they lived in, although 50% of those living at home also stated that domestic work was done by someone else. Complex negotiations, and sometimes conflicts, between these financial and domestic elements meant that most young adults were able to ensure some disposable income for leisure and going out.

Economic change has also had an effect on local communities in the North East. Many of those based on single industry and occupational homogeneity, have declined dramatically in economic as well as social terms. One well respected local commentator, Beatrix Campbell has highlighted the inwardly destructive response of some of these marginalised communities, particularly with reference to the conflict between displaced masculinity and men's involvement in criminality, and women's attempt to reassert values of caring and togetherness (Campbell, 1993). Our research shows that while local communities are certainly not dead, they do appear to be less important to young adults. For example, while neighbourhood friendships remain, few young people, particularly young women, choose to regularly socialise and have nights out in their local area.

These changes, although not quite so dramatic, also have an important bearing on the experiences university students, have regarding their involvement in youth cultures in the city. While higher education has traditionally provided middle class youth with a particular identity and a privileged bridge to the professional labour market, 'studentdom' can also be seen as a delayed transition, characterised by an experimentation with alternative values, shared living arrangements, and engagement in various leisure pursuits, including going out (Aggleton, 1987). Economic restructuring in the 1980s and 90s however, has meant a more general slow down in the economy, and many students, without parental connections, have come to expect unemployment as one of the main realities of graduation. Only 53% and 44% of graduates from Newcastle and Northumbria universities respectively were in permanent employment six months after leaving their institution (The Times Higher Education Supplement, May 27, 1994), and many of these would be non-graduate jobs.

Student's financial position during their tenure of study has also deteriorated dramatically over the last decade. For example, grants have shrunk with inflation over the years and government legislation designed to cut them by 10% each year over the next three years has recently been passed. Again, the domestic situation of students is also an important clue for comprehending how they balance income and expenditure, particularly in terms of consuming and going out (McCarthy and Humphrey, 1995). Living together in student areas has allowed for lower cost accommodation and splitting bills, with cost sharing in the leisure and consumption field involving a fairly complex system of borrowing. Socially, household sharing is also an important element of student culture in terms of cementing friendships, developing cultural identities and contouring leisure patterns.

The net effect of some of these changes are varied, although we would focus in on three issues in relation to students use of the city. First, while many remain convinced of the possibility of gaining access to the professional jobs market and are committed to the educational process, a section of the student population may be starting to question these expectations and opt to enjoy themselves socially by engaging in various youth cultural pursuits and activities. This U.K. version of 'Generation X' may involve the adoption of specific styles revolving around fashion, identity politics, sport or an attachment to particular music, drug or dance cultures. The second issue then is an increased differentiation amongst students themselves. And the final effect, concerns local reaction towards the expression of these various student lifestyles, cultures and communities and how this affects their use of the city.

If spheres such as work, educational destinations and traditional communities are declining as sources of stable identity, where do young adults express what and who they are? A number of theorist have raised the idea that young people are currently constructing themselves around these changing institutional fragments, developing a kind of 'patchwork' or post-modern identity (Redhead, 1993; O'Conner and Wynne, nd).[6] Another response might be that economic change has been responsible for the fact that consumption in the city has increasingly played an important role in identity formation. While this may be part of a general phenomenon, relating both to the experience of modernity and the economic and cultural importance cities have placed on developing a unique identity, it is particularly relevant for young adults. In an atmosphere of declining occupational and community based identities, and a rise in more global images and icons, the city is an ideal place for young people to reconcile tradition and change and literally re-create themselves.

The growing importance of the city as a site of social identity is also connected to a set of additional factors. First, it is a 'public space' in the sense that going out is a visible display of identity. Second, urban regeneration, in terms of leisure, public entertainment and the redevelopment of clubs and pubs, occurred in the same time frame as the region experienced its most rapid economic decline. And finally, this new consumption space did not readily discriminate against either students or the local population on the basis of age, class or gender criteria, and many young adults responded by appropriating sections of the city by claiming them as their own (Shields, 1991). The existence of these extended transitions and shifts in the sites whereby young people construct their identities, has had several significant and contradictory effects. One of the most important ones has been that the meaning and social context of going out has begun to be transformed from a simple 'rite of passage' to adulthood, towards a more permanent 'socialising' ritual for many young adults (Sande, 1994). In other words, involvement in youth cultures and nightlife rituals have simultaneously become a more central and stable aspect of identity formation, as well as created a space for activities, attitudes and behaviours which are neither youthful nor adult, but somewhere in between. Paradoxically, involvement in such cultures can both reflect and stand in for the loss of traditional identities, while also allowing young people to step outside of established roles and social expectations. A second effect then has been an increased fragmentation of youth identities and cultures in the contemporary period around issues of class, gender, race, sexuality, politics and consumption lifestyles (Featherstone, 1987). The ritualization of nights out has become, if you like, young adults' attempt to construct a modern equivalent of 'community', or more correctly, communities.

This movement from 'rites to rituals' signals an underlying change in the meaning and function of going out. While having a social life for students has always been part of their extended cultural transition, going out for locals historically was much more closely tied to 'growing up' and adulthood. Traditional rites revolved around courtship and marriage, introduction to alcohol, and integration into the community through the local pub. Drinking and going out in the North East was also embedded in a wider cultural apprenticeship based around masculinity and women's subordination in the home. Young men in particular were introduced to alcohol in a community setting by fathers or relatives and learnt to appreciate the taste of ale and acquired the capacity to hold their drink (Gofton, 1983). Their induction into the pub paralleled their transition into manual work and manhood generally- hence the traditional image of the hard-working, hard-drinking Geordie man. Women's subordinate role within this masculine occupational culture meant that they were largely limited to the private and domestic sphere, with the pub being primarily a male preserve. While there is evidence that some women did occupy some of these public spaces, like streets and pubs, their motivations were largely understood within the confines of domestic or sexual discourses (Common, 1951; McConville, 1983).

Clearly, the significance, meaning and wider social context surrounding youth cultures and going out has changed dramatically in the contemporary period (Gofton 1986; 1990). While certain aspects of these historical legacies survive and young people still initially enter into nightlife activities as a form of initiation into adulthood, it is readily apparent that the necessary social and economic conditions to make this wider transition are no longer secure. The decoupling of these processes has meant that going out can be engaged in for its own sake and need not be viewed as an element of growing up. Our research reveals that it increasingly has become an important and more permanent site of identity formation in its own right and is utilised by many young adults as a form of extended adolescence rather than a marker signifying adulthood.

Evidence supporting the view that going out has become a more central and significant aspect of personal identity for some young adults, is reflected in our findings concerning the frequency of nights out and the percentage of income spent on this activity. The shift of meaning and social context is exemplified clearly in terms of some of the obvious changes in nightlife culture like the fact that its is city and peer group-oriented rather than generationally transmitted and community-based. The increased presence of women and provision for students and the proliferation of youth cultures and styles also signal changes.

At the same time the changed meaning of going out is obscured somewhat by the continued use of traditional symbols like alcohol and assumptions that this activity is still motivated primarily by courtship rituals, even though sex has supposedly replaced marriage as the main driving force. While these remain important aspects of the activity, our research shows that socialising with friends and being part of a recognisable youth culture or style is increasingly becoming the primary 'raison detre' of having nights out. Furthermore, while the blockage or delay of transitions has meant that some young adults have sought to revive a version of a traditional local identity, by playing out what it means to be a 'Geordie' on city centre streets and pubs, others have sought to step outside dominant social expectations and roles and utilise this new found space to create different or alternative lifestyles.

One response by young adults designed to deal with economic restructuring, delayed transitions and the shift towards consumption, is to attempt to reinvent what it means to be a Geordie. In other words, for many youngsters, regional identity has less to do with work and industrial production and more to do with consumption in the city. However, the forms through which some young locals express themselves on a night out while contemporary, may attempt to reproduce elements of a 'mythical' collective past (Colls and Lancaster, 1992). For example, if young adults can never be Geordies in a true occupational sense, such an identity can be derived from a selective borrowing of historical images and traits, which are then combined with present day experiences and realities in other spheres. Examples of this, come from young adults own recognition of attempts by others to rejuvenate elements of the industrial archetype through the image of the 'Geordie hard man'.[7]

Carl (L18)   *I seem to think it's a bit personified by some of the lads' drinking in the city centre, this stereotypical Geordie bloke, Geordie town, where you have to be hard, you have to drink twenty pints, you have to have a curry, hit a policeman, then go on the pull afterwards, you know.*

While the so called 'hard lads' are a minority response, the symbolic aspects of male Geordie culture extend far beyond the stereotype. In one sense we argue that elements of this reconstruction continue to affect the style and pattern of nights out for many young men, despite the fact that for the majority it is largely a stylistic ritual (for example see the Bigg Market case study in section five). At the same time, many misconceptions and much of the hype surrounding violence in the city confuses playful adoptions of some of these symbols with an undying commitment to masculine values and anti-social behaviour.

Shifts in the meaning and social context of going out have also changed fundamentally because of the dramatic increase of women in the city (Wilson, 1991). Our research reveals that women go out more frequently, would feel worse if restricted, and spend a higher percentage of their income on nights out than their male counterparts. Despite the persistence of historical and contemporary barriers (Blackie, 1993), they have made significant leaps forward in terms reforming their own identities in relation to the city, and have played a central role in promoting the socialising aspect of going out. While young women continue to be influenced by domestic and sexual ideologies, female solidarity in dance and drug cultures (Henderson, 1993) and 'ladies only' nights out are two examples of this changing context.

In fact, the loosening of traditional roles generally has resulted in an increased differentiation amongst young adults and created the conditions for a proliferation of more specific youth cultures. Many young people are utilising extended transitions to explore the possibilities of alternative identities around not only gender (Wilkinson, 1994), but also sexual orientation (Whittle, 1994), politics, education, not to mention a range of music, drug and dance based cultures (Merchant and MacDonald, 1994; Coffield and Gofton, 1994; Henderson, 1993). While elements of these cultures cross over into orientations towards work, education, and politics, one of the main shifts has been a move away from some of the more traditional and localised attitudes and behaviours towards the consumption of more global images and styles.

The phenomenon of 'going out' is not then, we would argue, a frivolous activity only to be enjoyed, but is increasingly becoming a more central element in the production of contemporary youth identities. The changed meaning and social significance of this activity is reflected in the general movement from a 'rites to rituals', and this transformation while creating upheaval and often misinterpretation, also hints at future possibilities. To return to the quote at the beginning of this section, as Angela McRobbie (1993) has argued, 'youth remains a major symbolic investment for society as a whole', and this is why youth cultures in the city will be of continuing interest in the years to come. In the sections which follow, we question some of myths concerning nights out, attempt to put various rituals and cultures into a social context and make some relevant urban policy suggestions.

'Going out for Geordies...its like a religion' (Assistant Pub Manager in the Bigg Market)

'Quite suicidal' (a female student when asked how she would feel if restricted from going out for 3 months)

4. Findings

Prevalence and importance of going out

The strength of our research findings and overall thesis about the growing significance of going out hinges on the prevalence and importance young adults ascribe to nights out. Overall, our total sample of sixty individuals had been going out to pubs, clubs and/or music venues in the city centre an average of 8.6 times per month for a period of 4.5 years. As such, our research findings are drawn from experiences gained from over a cumulative total of 270 years and over 22,000 visits to Newcastle city centre[8].

Within these overall figures, two further points are noteworthy. First, our student cohort went out to the city centre an average of 10.5 times per month, while locals averaged 6.8 visits per month. The difference is perhaps partly explained by the culture of student life, flexible schedules and their greater access to cash through overdrafts and loans. Second, in the case of both locals and students, it is interesting to note that women actually go out more frequently to the city centre in the evening than their male counterparts. This is particularly surprising in the case of locals, where it is obvious that women have a much lower level of weekly income than men. Additionally, these findings generally contradict a range of research which shows that young women continue to have lower participation rates in organised leisure and a heavier involvement in domestic labour, not to mention the gender specific issue of sexual harassment in the city.

When one adds night time visits to pubs and clubs in either their own area or other areas of Newcastle to the figures above, the total number of nights out rises for the whole sample to an average of 11.2 visits per month. Again, students continue to go out more frequently overall, with the majority of visits occurring in their own neighbourhoods, namely areas like Fenham, Jesmond and Heaton.

However, it is Geordie men who utilise these local spaces the most, which places them ahead of local women with respect to overall nights out. Clearly, the 'community pub' retains some importance for students and local men, while local women appear to be largely absent here (73% did not use them regularly), choosing nights out in the city centre instead. Over half of our sample also went on nights out to pub/ clubs and music venues outside of Newcastle but still in the North East, and 60% had visited another city specifically to have a night out.

While these prevalence rates themselves lend some support to the centrality of going out in young adults lives, two other findings are also illuminating in this regard. First, we asked our sample how they would feel if they were indeed restricted from going out for a period of three months. Nearly 90% of our respondents said they would feel 'bad' or 'very bad' if this were the case. More emotive responses such as **'devastated', 'gutted', 'it would kill us'** were the norm. Again, students were most likely to say that they would feel 'very bad' if restricted and young local women were also more likely to say this when compared to their male counterparts.

Second, it is possible, by comparing incomes and spending patterns, to estimate the proportion of material wealth devoted to nights out (see the next sub-section for more details). Our sample claimed to spend 38% of their total income on evenings out in the city centre only. It is important to note that this figure does not include local visits or expenditure on clothes, make-up, toiletries, hair care, shoes or drugs. Alternatively, these percentage figures for spending may be inflated somewhat due to the amount of borrowing that goes on.

Students claimed to spend 44% of their income on nights out, although according to other research (McCarthy and Humphrey, 1995), our cohort appear to have underestimated their weekly income level. After adjusting the figures, students still appear to spend nearly 30% of their income on this activity. Overall, locals spent a similar percentage of their weekly income on nights out, with young men spending a quarter and young women spending 37% of their earnings. High prevalence rates, combined with young adults' significant material investment in and expressed desire to have nights out, demonstrates the important role this activity plays in their everyday life.

Spending and income

As we have argued, the amount of money young adults spend going on nights out as a proportion of their total income, indicates the relative importance they attribute to this activity. A further breakdown of spending patterns also helps to give substance to some of the main patterns of going out as well as highlighting some of the more specific activities young people engage in.

The average weekly amount of money our overall sample had to spend was approximately £75. Of the various subgroups the most well off (relatively) was local men (£102 per week), followed by student women (£73), local women (£70) and student men (£64). Employed local men earned approximately £144 per week, while local working women averaged £105. Income levels clearly do have an influence on whether young adults felt restricted from going out more often. Local men, for example were the group least likely to feel that their income prevented them from going out when they wanted to (only 27% said this). Nearly half of local women felt their income restricted them from going out, while 70% of students felt this (male students were most likely to say this).

However, there was a significant contradiction between this feeling of being restricted and actual behaviour with regard to spending. For instance, while most likely to feel restricted, student men in the sample actually spent the most as a percentage of their claimed income. They were followed in descending order by student women, local women and finally local men. Part of the explanation lies of course with disparities in income. However, it was also clear that the decision to sacrifice a fairly substantial proportion of one's income depends partly on the desire to go out, not to mention the fact that students were more able to rely on additional sources of funding. The use of a complex system of borrowing by both students and locals also helps to explain this apparent paradox.

For example, over 80% of our sample had borrowed money to go out on a night out with little difference existing between locals and students. The major variation was that locals were much more likely to report that they borrowed from their parents, while students appeared to rely heavily on their friends and house-mates. As such, the latter group was also more apt to have to pay this money back, presumably due to the fact that their lender was also likely to be a financially insecure student, while some locals relied on the goodwill of parents (still two-thirds had to pay this money back). Finally, while students paid their own way, 20% of locals actually reported that someone else paid for their night out. Local men in this category were likely to be unemployed, under 18, living at home and financed by their parents, while a small percentage of local women relied either on husbands or boyfriends for their nights out.

On a given night out the big spender was local men who splashed out on average £17.70, reflecting not only their higher disposable income but perhaps a stronger cultural attachment to the one big weekend night out. While this was an average figure for going out, combining pubs with clubs often ran the total bill up to £30-40, but these types of visits were made less frequently. Considering their lower income and the fact that they drink less, local women were not far behind, spending £16.50 per night out. Student men spent on average £14 and student women £11.50, reflecting perhaps lower prices in the union bars and special student nights. However, on a weekly basis, due to differences in the number of times they go out, this order is almost entirely reversed with student men spending the most, followed by student women, with local men and women spending almost equal amounts.

While it is difficult to get an exact breakdown of spending patterns, it was possible to gather some general information on the various financial components making up a night out. The vast majority of money spend on a night out for most of our sample was on drink, with 97% percent spending money on alcohol. Over 80% of our sample spent money on entrance fees to clubs, while 79% spent money on transport (taxi, Metro or bus), 45% paid out on food and 23% bought cigarettes. Students were more likely to pay out money to get into clubs, while locals were more apt to spend money on food and taxis. Twenty percent of our overall sample actually bought drugs at a pub or club and clearly a higher percentage than this bought drugs prior to a night out.

To conclude, while income levels clearly do exert some restrictions on spending, most young adults engage in various forms of 'creative accounting' in order to enjoy nights out. It is equally the case however, that there are financial limits to parental generosity, borrowing and overdrafts and the continued success of the night time service economy is obviously dependent on the overall growth and development of the region's economic fortunes, not to mention student grant levels.

The divided city

The notion of the 'divided city' has a long history in urban sociology[9] and was a key idea in the formulation of this research project. We would define the divided city simply as the process whereby different sections of the population inhabit city space and construct lifestyles which both assert their own identity, and which may act to exclude or dissuade other groups from encroaching on their territory and culture.

In this section of the report we are particularly concerned to explore social divisions between locals and students, the effects of unemployment and economic polarisation, the position of women in the city, and the curtailment of groups based on their race or sexual orientation.

Table Three provides some evidence of the differential use of city space on nights out by locals and students in Newcastle. The main divisions would appear to be the latter group's lower presence in the Bigg Market and their much higher use of the University (student unions) and Station areas. The main area of convergence would appear to be the Haymarket, although comparable rates of use of other areas include the Riverside and Gallogate. The Quayside is also clearly the most popular area with students with 60% saying they use it regularly and it is also a significant nightspot for many locals. Generally student use across the board is higher than the local group, expressing the fact that they go out more frequently and perhaps use a wider range of night-time facilities.

It might be argued that these figures play down the amount of segregation between locals and students by not accounting for the fact that these groups may visit different pubs in the same area, or use the same areas on different nights. There is a well recognised distinction between local and 'studentish' pubs, for example in the Haymarket area, and various pub guides and university handbooks help to reinforce such demarcations elsewhere. To account for this we asked our sample to describe the clientele of the places they frequent regularly as well as to specify the main nights they utilised the city centre. Sixty percent of Geordies went to pubs, clubs and music venues described as 'local', one third used mixed places, with only 7% going to 'mostly student' places. Half of all students went to 'student venues', 40% attended mixed venues and 10% went out to 'local' places. One of the reasons why there may be slightly more mixing amongst the student grouping is their higher attendance at clubs and music venues which tend to attract a more diverse crowd.

27

TABLE THREE

AREAS OF THE CITY USED REGULARLY ON NIGHTS OUT

(Expressed as a Percentage of the Sample*)

	LOCALS			STUDENTS		
	Total	Men	Women	Total	Men	Women
Haymarket	50	53	47	50	53	47
Bigg Market	50	67	33	30	33	27
Quayside	43	20	67	60	60	60
Riverside	20	33	7	17	27	7
Central**	13	13	13	23	13	33
Station	3	-	7	33	53	13
Gallowgate	7	13	-	7	7	7
University	-	-	-	27	40	13

*   Respondents may use more than one area of the city regularly

**   Refers to the area around John Dobson St and the Monument

As mentioned, student use of areas like the Haymarket, Quayside and Bigg Market may actually occur on different nights than that of locals. Despite the fact that only just over fifty percent of young Geordies are tied to a 'working week' the vast majority tend to reserve going out on a Friday and Saturday night. Very few locals go out regularly on a Monday and Tuesday, with a slow build up as the weekend approaches. Students, on the other hand, while engaging in the traditional Friday night, are actually more apt to attend 'student specials' on Mondays and go out through the week, than use the city centre on Saturday. As one undergraduate respondent put it, *'We tend to leave the city to Geordies on Saturday night...students are more likely to stay in and have house parties or go to their local pub'.*

While local/ students divisions are apparent, it is important not to over-emphasise differences. For example, it is unhelpful to stereotype either population as it is worth noting that as many local people utilise the Haymarket area of the city as the Bigg Market and nearly as many use the Quayside. Furthermore, it is obvious that there is a significant gender difference amongst the local population as to the use of different areas. Local women for instance were much more likely to use the Quayside (67%) and the Haymarket (47%) rather than the Bigg Market (33%) and their pattern of use mirrors student trends more than that of their male counterparts. And even though the Bigg Market appears to be the favourite of local men, they too made good use of other areas, particularly the Haymarket. Clearly, there are sections of each of these populations who choose to avoid one another, while there are others who feel perfectly comfortable in each others company. There are areas of the city where students and locals do meet, and there are examples of mixing around particular pubs, clubs, and music venues.

These variable patterns might partly explain the ambivalence both groups have in assessing local/ student relations in the city. Both populations are divided as to whether they see relations as 'bad', 'good' or 'indifferent'. Only 20% of locals and 23% of students thought relations were actually good, while 33% and 30% respectively thought they were bad. Most agreed however, that animosity is created largely by a minority section of each of the respective populations (see **Transcribed Interviews** 1).

Although not always directly articulated, much of the conflict reflects class differences between the populations, represented by accent, dress codes, general attitudes and apparent material wealth. A number of students from the North West (Manchester and Liverpool) and Scotland, felt personally that there was more affinity between themselves and Geordies, and that locality and accent were important intervening factors in establishing good relations. Additionally, even more students raised the archetypal loud 'southern' speaking, rugby-playing, private school student, as the one who would raise the most hackles. Some locals were critical of student privileges and attitudes, while others berated the small mindedness of their own communities. The important point is that our research did not reveal many serious physical altercations between students and locals and there were examples of where these groups happily mixed and co-existed.

The city may also become divided when unemployment and poverty act to exclude sections of the local population from participating in the night time economy. As revealed in **Table One** earlier, nearly one-sixth of our sample of local young adults were classed as unemployed. One of the main class constraints concerning young people's leisure is the lack of a proper wage and those in the 16-17 year old category, unable to claim income support, are particularly vulnerable to the effects of economic and social polarisation. Local research suggests that exclusion may result in some young people becoming trapped in

TRANSCRIBED INTERVIEWS 1

STUDENT-LOCAL RELATIONS IN NEWCASTLE

Locals:

Jan (L29) — *The people who drink in my bars work, and they hate people who don't work, which is students. I'll tell you where they really hate them, in the local pubs, like in the X (in Walker), they hate students, they absolutely detest them. They think they're a complete waste of time, such a working class, 'What the hell you need to gan' to college for', type of thing, grow up and get in the real world. They can't abide like, nineteen, twenty, twenty-one year olds, who've never had a job basically.*

Carl (L18) — *I mean I get seen as a student [he is at Newcastle College] when I was walking through town the other night. Up towards the Poly there was about five of these kind of hard lads near the side kind of shouted,' We're paying for your beer you fucking student', I said, 'yea, cos I'm cleverer than you'. I got chased all the way home.*

Students:

Bob (S22) — *I haven't had any trouble whatsoever, all the locals I have ever spoken to have been perfectly friendly to me. There just seems to be an affinity between the locals here and the people from Liverpool, they always seem to be able to relate to each other, obviously a lot to do with the histories of the cities and what sort of people they are, and their interests.*

Anne (S22) — *Em, I think it depends really, there's a lot of the stigma that people in Newcastle and like Sunderland and places hate students, and you do find this quite a bit. But they tend to be more like townies sort of types tend to think that. But em, if you go to clubs, like you'll go to a club and there are people there whether they are students or locals who have got the same interest in going out, having a good time, they're not going to hassle you.*

Mick (S21) — *It is just because most of the students are loud and obnoxious, and if you're a local, you're not going to put up with a sort of eighteen year old kids, away from home for the first time, sort of...... in your face. Also because it seems the students have got a lot of money as well, so that is going to be, I don't know, there is not a lot of money up here for the locals, they are going to see students spending money, and they'll not like it. I've seen students get punched and stuff, but it's probably their own fault for being stupid.*

30

their own marginalised communities, and young males in particular may turn to criminal activity and drug use as alternative sources of identity (Campbell, 1993).[10]

Our research partly supports the point that economic marginalisation does affect involvement in the socialising function of going out, particular amongst this young group. Those out of work do find their lack of money restricting in terms of having nights out and they may compensate by going out less frequently, experience longer periods of being homebound, or decide going out to the city centre is too expensive or not a spending priority. This was particularly the case with a number of young men who were unable to claim income support:

Pete (L16)   *Cos' ave never got money, like an odd tenner off me ma' and da'an' that but still not enough. If yer gan oot with a tenner, ya' knaa what a mean, to toon, you git about four pints, then you're skint, yer haven't got yer taxi fare. The high streets much cheaper. Then the social clubs are like one pound two pence for a pint of McEwans, ya' knaa. Dead cheap in there.*

Other young adults who had established a pattern of going out, continued to do so despite becoming unemployed. Part of the explanation for this phenomenon is that nights out for some young adults may provide an even more important socialising function and source of identity in the absence of work. This was made possible by altering some of the patterns of going out (drinking less, happy hours, going straight to a club) and by relying on many of the same mechanisms as their employed counterparts such as living at home, helping out with domestic work, relying on parental generosity and borrowing from friends. Overall then, our research revealed that despite financial restrictions, the majority of unemployed youth did continue to go out albeit less frequently.

The idea of the divided city received a new impetus in the 1970s and 80s with the development of various feminist insights in sociology and human geography (Mackenzie, 1989). Most explanations concerning the position of women in cities are derived from the concept of 'patriarchy', which has been defined as: 'the institutional all encompassing power that men have as a group over women, the systematic exclusion of women from power in society and the systematic devaluation of all roles and traits that society has assigned to women' (Popkin in Aggleton, 1990). While feminist theory has different strands and is not a unified body of thought, most theories of patriarchy focus on the relationship between economic, domestic and cultural factors (i.e. representations of sexuality).

The notion of the divided city by gender is predicated on the effect these various factors have on the organisation and separation of urban areas into public (male) and private (female) spaces. For example, women's subordinate economic and domestic position mean that they have less resources with which to enjoy the city, not to mention how their responsibility for domestic labour limits time and energy for leisure. The representation of women culturally as 'sex objects' also means that those who do venue out may be subject to sexual violence and harassment. Our research findings support aspects of this kind of analysis. For example, local women earned roughly 30% less than their male counterparts, found their income more restricting in terms of nights out and were more apt to have to contribute to domestic labour in the household. Furthermore, they were more likely to say there were parts of the city they would not use, including their local communities, and had a greater chance of being personally involved in violence than local men. Along with student women, 60% of the female sample also suggested they had been subject to sexual harassment on a night out.

At the same time, there is growing evidence that many young women are beginning to cross the public/private divide. Critiques of traditional feminism as too deterministic and the advent of 'power feminism' in the U.S. (Wolfe, 1994), has led to a reconsideration of their changed position, or at least changing attitudes, particularly amongst young women. Elizabeth Wilson (1991), for instance, has suggested 'Yet the city, a place of growing threat and paranoia to men, might be a place of liberation for women'. While somewhat overstated, again some of our research findings lend support to the growing power and presence of women in the city. Women go out more frequently to the city centre, would feel worse if restricted from going out and spend a higher percentage of their income on nights out than men. Class differences also appear to play a part role here. Student women, who are more likely to be middle class, are the single most active group in terms of the frequency of going out and less likely than local women to say there were dangerous areas or parts of the city they would not use. They were also less likely to have experienced sexual harassment or violence on a night out. Yet as our case study of 'ladies only' nights out demonstrates (see section five), young working class women are also developing various strategies to make their presence felt on city centre streets. The issue of the gender divided city then is based not only on economic and domestic restrictions, but also concerns young women's desire for freedom and safety within the night time economy. Finally, the idea of the divided city can be used to refer to issues of outright exclusion and discrimination. In this regard we asked our sample to comment on two particular aspects concerning accessibility- the issue of ethnicity and racism and views on the provision of night-time facilities and space for gays and lesbians (see **Transcribed Interviews 2** for comments).

Census data for 1991 shows that 95.9% of Newcastle's population is classified as white. The largest grouped category after this is Pakistani/ Indian/ Asian (2.3%), followed by Chinese (0.5%), Bagladeshi (0.5%), Black African/ Carribean (0.4%) and an Other category (0.4%). This breakdown by percentage of the population reflects, to some extent, our sample's perceptions of what was meant by the areas 'ethnic minorities', even though one should be careful to distinguish between subgroups within these general categories. The so called 'Asian population', which is really a misnomer, is largely recognised in relation to their segregation to certain areas of the city on the basis of housing (i.e. Fenham, Elswick), while the Chinese are seen more in terms of their business activities in the city centre (i.e. Chinatown). Finally, the very small number of Black African/ Carribeans in the area, may be offset partly by the high profile nature of Newcastle United players like Ruel Fox and the now departed Andy Cole. Ironically, while the success and popularity of these players was initially held up as a leap forward in race relations in the city, privately it was recently revealed that their own families and friends were subject to racial abuse on Tyneside.

We asked our sample whether or not they felt that Newcastle's young ethnic minorities had access to the city centre in the evening, partly to solicit their views, but also to invite general comments on the issue. Our local sample was evenly divided on the issue with 40% saying the city was accessible to ethnic minorities, while 40% felt it was not (20% said they didn't know). Students were much less likely to say that it was accessible, with only 17% answering in the affirmative.

For those who felt it was accessible, the main reason given was their experience of seeing ethnic minority groups using the city centre in the evening (both Asian and Afro Carribean and to a lesser extent

Accessibility for Ethnic Groups on 'Nights Out':

Carey (L31)   *You don't see many, but there is a huge Asian population, so I mean, where do they go? The town musn't be giving them whatever it is they would like to have. So they obviously don't have any choice, its either what we like or nowt.*

Gema (S21)   *I suppose it should be accessible, if they want to go to the city centre they have got every right, but I don't think so no. Especially not the Bigg Market, there's a lot of prejudice and racism.*

Nadim (L24)   *I don't think there's any problems. I mean I've never had any problems. I mean the fact of being coloured doesn't make any difference in the Bigg Market and that.*

Dee (L21)   *They completely contradict themselves, because they see sort of like a big group of say Pakistani people walking and its have a go at them. Not to their faces or anything, but the comments will start. But then they see like a great big black, really black man, say on a Friday night, and they say 'Isn't he cool, you know what I mean, and they sort of worship that person.*

Provision of Nightlife Facilities for Gays and Lesbians:

Natalie (S22)   *I never hear any complaints that there aren't enough nights for gay people. But at the same time there doesn't seem to be that many venues or nights for them really. But I know when Speak Easy was open, that seemed to go down really well, because there was a mix, it was like fifty fifty of gays and straight people and it went really well, everyone had a really good time, we used to love it there, then that closed down.*

Andy (S22)   *I think the er, going, I think in the Bigg Market it is very much of a male oriented environment which would, if I was gay, would put me off.*

Gary (L29)   *I think there should be a section for gay people, and a section for er, er, normal people you know, wrong choice of word, I know (...) if you go into a gay club and then someone tries to try it on then you could end up.... say you're out with your three mates and you go into a club, and you didn't know it was a gay club, and you had guys trying to try it on, then there's going to be trouble you know.*

34

Chinese youth), and a failure to recall any incidents of racial harassment there. This view is at least partly supported by the fact that there were no actual racist attacks reported by our sample which occurred in the city centre during a night out. That proportion of the sample who stated that they 'did not know' if the city centre was accessible, raised the issue of whether ethnic minorities actually would want to use this public space.

While locals were more apt to see their city as accessible when compared to students, a significant proportion of our sample was convinced that Newcastle nightlife didn't exactly provide a welcoming environment for ethnic minorities. The main reason given was racism, expressed not so much as attacks or specific incidents, but rather as a general attitude. This was sometimes linked to the fact that the region is largely white and that Geordie culture, by its very nature, is somewhat exclusionary. As evidence, ten percent of the local sample itself expressed what might be considered to be racist remarks in response to the question of ethnic accessibility, with the majority of views being directed against the Asian population by young men.

The debate over whether racism is more prevalent in predominantly white localities like Tyneside as opposed to mixed inner cities is difficult to assess (Bonnett, 1993). Furthermore, one should not automatically assume from these findings that racism is more predominate amongst the local population, and rife in particular areas of the city centre catering for them (like the Bigg Market), and that other areas are safe and students are somehow 'anti-racist' simply because they appear to be more aware of the problem. The question is not whether ethnic minorities in Newcastle experience racism, but rather where incidents occur, how it is expressed and whom it is directed towards.

Finally, the notion of the divided city was explored in relation to the provision of night-time facilities for gays and lesbians and views surrounding the issue of gay space and segregation. While there is an emerging space for gay nightlife in Newcastle, known informally as the 'Pink Triangle', there is not yet an equivalent to Manchester's higher profile and more long-standing 'Gay Village'. Not surprisingly then, a high percentage of our respondents did not know whether Newcastle provided for its gay and lesbian population (45% of the overall sample said this). Of the quarter who did feel that there were adequate facilities, the majority did so on the basis of being able to name particular clubs and pubs as being 'exclusively gay' or as having gay nights. And while the final 30% felt that this groups' needs were not being met, they too at least were able to identify particular gay venues in the city.

The main issue then was not really whether the city adequately catered for gay and lesbian needs, but whether it should and how this would be most effectively achieved (see **Transcribed Interviews 2** for comments). There are a number of contrasting perspectives on this question which in some sense reflect debates within the gay community itself (see the case study in section five), while others represent variations of a wider heterosexual ideology. For instance, there is the argument that the development of identifiable gay areas and venues is an expression of growing power and organisation amongst this section of the population. In this view, stress is placed on the fact that there is a need for a space where gays and lesbians can feel relaxed and comfortable with their lifestyle and sexuality, free from the pressures and constraints of the 'mainstream' heterosexual society. The idea of a strictly 'gay only' admissions policy might be seen as an example of this position. There is however a counter view which suggests that this leads to a form of social segregation or 'apartheid', pushing gay culture to the margins of the city as it were.

Variations of these positions are held by different sections of the heterosexual community. For example, the proportion of our sample who could be described as 'pro gay', in the sense of supporting the right to adopt this lifestyle, often slipped between these two positions. While they welcomed the development of a gay village in terms of providing the community with a safe space, they also expressed concern with its effect on reinforcing the exclusion of these groups elsewhere. A different heterosexual response saw segregation as a positive thing, mainly because they believed that it was the best way for groups to get on and reduce conflict. A minority of the sample was explicitly anti-gay and argued against any provision for this group.

The notion of the divided city is an important one and is central to the issue of differentiation amongst young adults, as well raises questions of inequality and exclusion. For the most part, we have limited our comments primarily to the general findings of our survey and to the social context behind these issues. In a later sub-section on widening access, we discuss some of the general policy implications of these social divisions.

Initiation

Like all cultural rites, going out involves a process of experimentation and learning which one might refer to as initiation. A lack of knowledge and familiarity with the social rules concerning this activity can often result in embarrassment or anxiety for the individual involved and sometimes manifest itself as a wider social problem. Most of our respondents had very vivid memories of their early experiences of going out and we base much of our discussion here on their recollections.

It has been suggested previously that young people's introduction to the local culture of drinking and going out took place largely within the family and community and was highly contoured by the wider masculine occupational culture. Learning how to hold one's drink was an important symbol signifying the movement from youthfulness to adulthood, particularly for young men. More recently it has been argued that initiation rites take place largely in the peer group, and are no longer tied so closely to either gender or a specified rite of passage into the adult world (Gofton, 1990). This change has sometimes resulted in charges that many young people are learning 'inappropriate' behaviours in this sphere. While our research supports the general view that there has been a historical shift in the social context of going out, our analysis offers up a slightly different explanation for this transition which avoids an implicit social problem model and stresses that some continuities with past patterns remain.

National statistics show that the majority of young people are introduced to alcohol in their own and other family households around the age of 13 (Marsh et al, 1986). The average age of our sample when they first went out to have a drink was 15.4 years, the same for locals and students. The vast majority of these first visits were to pubs rather than nightclubs and outing were primarily spontaneous and sporadic. The majority did not start to go out regularly until 17 or 18 for a variety of reasons including being under-age, a lack of money or too busy with school work.

Half of our local sample had their first drink in a public establishment in either their local community or in a surrounding area of Newcastle. Less than a third actually had their first night out in the city centre itself, and of this latter group the majority were initiated by older sisters, brothers or cousins, rather than by their peer group. The idea that initiation into the world of going out has been corrupted by under-age visits to the city accompanied only by one's peers, ignores the fact that a family type apprenticeship still does occur and early experiences of drinking are more likely to take place in the home and community.

Not surprisingly then, the majority of our local sample stated that their first night out in Newcastle city centre was a good experience, with only 10% saying they had a bad first night. Most were exhilarated by the sheer number of people out, the variety of places to go to and the general hustle and bustle of the city. While a minority might have experienced some personal problems or embarrassing social situations, most remembered these with a certain degree of humour:

Lynn (L29)   *I went out when I was fifteen with me sister who was seventeen at the time, and em, I didn't know what to wear so she got us dressed, she put me make-up on, she did me hair, I was wearing me mam's clothes. We went to a disco pub which used to be called Grobbs. She had been going out quite a while, we only stayed out an hour, then she brought us home, cos I had embarrassed her so much. I didn't act mature enough. It was something to look back on and laugh at.*

In addition to learning a range of appropriate skills and behaviours necessary to have a good night out, for example how to get quick service, getting by bouncers, and how to avoid conflict or trouble, local young people also begin to develop specific habits, patterns and routes around the city centre, many of which stay with them into their late 20s. These habits include group drinking, pub hopping according to a set route, round buying and interacting with members of the opposite sex. One of the reasons why some of these early patterns remain relates to the fact that their economic and domestic situation may remain largely unchanged for an extended period, and behaviours once devised as rites become ritualised over time.

At the same time most of the young adults we interviewed recognised a shift in both their reasons for going out, the type of places they frequented, and what parts of the city they actually utilised. Two thirds of our local sample stated that they now went to places that were different than when they initially started going out. For example, there was a general perception that while under-age youngster went out primarily to meet someone of the opposite sex, young adults were much more engaged in an extended socialising ritual involving meeting old friends or making new ones. Additionally, there was a recognised move away or branching out from the Bigg Market bars, which were sometimes perceived as catering for the younger and more inexperienced set, to older, more 'up-market' or 'casual' pubs on the Quayside or in the Station area of the city. Students also go through a process of initiation which is used to confirm their collective identity. It is also central in cementing friendships groups as well as contouring their own patterns of behaviour and spacial use of the city on nights out. Again drink, and perhaps drug use, plays a central role in this process of initiation, even though like locals they have had previous experience of going out to pubs or clubs prior to coming to university. Despite this, initiation for many involved a relearning of drinking patterns and associated behaviour as part of their induction into student life during 'Freshers Week'. One individuals' recollection of this week highlights some of the main features of this initiation:

Cal (S26)   *We tried to get into various places full of bouncers and whatever, and I think when you first go to college you do tend to go out with people that you get thrown together with, and then you meet other people, and you stop going out with those people and I think it was that kind of experience, and I was still really learning about, although I was a bit older by then. I didn't have much experience of what I would call, serious drinking, so I think I found the amount of alcohol that was being consumed by the people quite daunting at that time.*

Again the issue of learning inappropriate drinking behaviours and habits arises. Becoming a university student is of course an officially sanctioned extension of youthfulness. While some students may engage in exactly the same behaviours that are condemned in an area like the Bigg Market, they have the advantage of those activities being seen as 'high spirited' fun, in addition to them taking place in a private space (the union) with internal policing (i.e. the university police). One local male in first year university critically compared one of the student union bars with the city centre:

RH	Would you say that it (the union) is wilder than places down the Bigg Market?
Geoff(L21)	In a totally different way though. It is not wild really, I know they are pulling their trousers down, but if you put them down the Bigg Market, they would never do that. They do it up there because they know they will get away with it. They are doing it because, well I mean chronic immaturity is one thing. You see in the Bigg Market, you get a lot less silly behaviour, but if you overstep the mark, you know with some dodgy character you can get seriously hurt. But you don't often see people squatting on a table you know, crapping on it and things like that you know, which is what has happened up there and stuff like that, it just doesn't happen. Because also no boy in his like seventy quid white shirt that he's been saving up for, and his nice slacks and whatever, is going to want to pull his strides down, you know what I mean. He is out there trying to impress the women, some lass down the Bigg Market is going to gan' 'Eee, what's he doing', he is just going to get his head kicked in. But up there it's like, 'Oh, well done Bartholomew the rugby player'.

Student's re-introduction to drinking and going out initially takes place around the university unions and various carefully routed pub crawls, and handbooks highlight student friendly pubs. Initiation rites for students then are an important factor in establishing later patterns for going out and in reinforcing the divided city. However some begin to move away the confines of the university fairly early on and start to explore city nightlife more in terms of their musical tastes, peer group interests and youth cultural affiliations.

To conclude, while we would agree that initiation rites can result in specific troublesome incidents, our findings contradict the idea that older local patterns have completely disappeared or that changes that have taken place automatically imply an increase in social disorder. We would argue instead that the fundamental reasons for change lies in the social conditions undergirding the creation of an 'extended' adolescence, for both locals and students, and the attraction of the city as a plausible site of identity in place of traditional sources. Young adults may be engaging in 'youthful' behaviours much longer not because of the corrupting influence of the city, but because the conditions for growing up are no longer there.

The social meaning of going out

Early criticism of this research revolved largely around the fact that the social meaning of going out is self-evident. While not wanting to completely discount elements of common sense, it should be clear that meanings are closely tied up with the social context in which they occur and that this backdrop is not always readily observable. Additionally, we argue that the meaning of going out has altered significantly in relation to wider economic and cultural transformations.

Evidence that the social context has indeed changed was strongly supported by the social meanings our respondents attached to going out. **Table Four** sets out the cumulative total of the three main reasons people gave for why they went on nights out. The two predominate meanings our overall sample gave to explain what going out means to them were an emotional or subjective characteristic (with 73% saying this), and socialising with friend (62%). Getting drunk or high was distant third (35%), followed by going out to dance or listen to music (25%) and just meeting people (20%). Surprisingly, only 18% gave meeting potential sexual partners, as one of the three main reasons why they went out. The same percentage said it was a relief from work or education, while 10% stated they simply wanted to get out of the house.

The idea that the social context and meaning of going out has changed significantly perhaps helps to explain these findings, some of which might contradict common sense views on this subject. For example, our argument that going out has become less of a rite of passage from youthfulness to adulthood and more a permanent fraternisation ritual, supports the idea that the meaning of nights out for people has shifted away from some of its traditional functions to become more of a permanent way of life in terms of socialising within one's own post-adolescent community. While young people may continue to use nights out to signal their movement into adulthood (i.e. the celebration of ones 18th birthday), evidence of the changing nature of their social condition is reflected by the ritualization and extension of this activity to include 21st, 25th and even 30th and 40th birthdays!

41

THE SOCIAL MEANING OF GOING OUT

		Locals		Students	
	Total	Men	Women	Men	Women
Emotional/ psychological	73%	67%	73%	73%	80%
Socialise with friends	62%	40%	87%	47%	53%
Get drunk	35%	47%	53%	7%	33%
Dance/ music	25%	13%	13%	33%	40%
Meet people	20%	-	20%	20%	40%
Break from work/ studies	18%	-	7%	33%	33%
Meet opposite sex	18%	47%	13%	13%	-
Get out of house	10%	27%	7%	7%	-

This shift partly explains the significance young adults attribute to socialising with friends on nights out. Locals in particular stressed this aspect, but students also displayed this sense of 'groupness' and wider feeling of sociability:

Roy (L21)   *Socialising and having fun. Um...just a...meet the lads, like, have a laugh and that, a daft carry on, let your hair down. Just see a lotta people, see people from school an that, that you haven't seen for a long time. There's a lotta people that go down the town to see them and that.*

Lee (S19)   *Everybody from the house went out, and a lad from the house had all his friends down from Manchester, they all came out. It was the week before Christmas actually, and my friends were all up from Manchester so they all came out with me and we met everybody off the course, and we went to the Boat. There were about twenty or more of us, and it was just excellent, and then everybody came back to ours and like smoking session, drinking session, carried on, we were just up till all hours of the morning, it was really good.*

In conducting this research we were struck by the importance of friendships and group solidarity on nights out. Many local respondents were willing to undergo debt and conflict with family members and partners in order to go out regularly with their gang on a Friday night. People's recollection of their best night out often revolved around the atmosphere created through going out in the company of a large group of friends. The significance of nights out as a socialising circle, was also underlined by the fact that groups members were more likely to have met one another in pubs/ clubs as they were to have been workmates. Close-knit groups also organised around musical tastes, dance and clothing styles or through student circles. The primary 'raison detre' of these 'mini-communities' was companionship and fraternisation achieved through an engagement in ritualised activity over extended periods of time.

The importance of explaining the meaning of going out in terms of emotional and subjective categories also relates to a changing social context. While going out has always contained an air of excitement, it has been argued that economic uncertainty, rapid social change and the experience of modernity has resulted in the emergence of new 'risk cultures' amongst young people (Beck, 1992).[11] Some of these cultures might be described as the quest for excitement in an unexciting world and the role of the city as a site for this experience may be important here. Many of our respondents used terms like *'getting a buzz', 'experiencing the crack', 'letting your hair down', 'being in with a crowd'* to explain the experience of going out. Responses like 'getting out of the house' and 'relief from work and education' also fit into this notion of relieving boredom and monotony.

The role of drink is also connected with the idea of socialising rituals, as well as risk cultures. Alcohol, as the anthropologist Mary Douglas (1987) reminds us, literally creates community. However, its social significance lies not so much now as a rite of passage into the adult community, but rather as a an extended ritual signifying one's membership into a intermediate zone of 'post-adolescence'. Drinking, and increasingly drug use, in this sense becomes less of a transition rite and more a ritual signalling this separate phase of life. As such young adults can continue to engage elements of the rite such as over-indulgence, combine it with symbolic aspects of a kind of risk culture ('live for today' attitude), and ritualise both as a permanent feature of a Friday night 'booze up' or 'getting high'.

Finally, a quick word need to be said about the relative lack of importance our respondents attributed to meeting a potential partner on nights out. Again, we would attempt to explain this apparent anomaly with reference to the wider changing social context. For instance, while one of the central purposes of going out in the past may have been to look for a potential wife or husband, the economic, domestic and social conditions many young adults have inherited completely discount this as a possibility. Other transformations, such as the changing position of women and health risks associated with AIDS and HIV may have also altered perceptions on this matter. These, and other factors, may have combined to produce a much more relaxed atmosphere on nights out which revolves more around socialising and less around sexual conquest. All this is not to say that sexual matters are unimportant for young adults. However, there appears to be a disjuncture between the symbolic display and verbalisation of sexuality expressed in language, dress codes, glances and posturing, and to paraphrase the Coke commercial, 'the real thing'.

Routes and patterns

The ritual of going out is reinforced by a series of set patterns of behaviour and the adoption of particular routes through the city centre. These include for instance, pre-night out activities, the idea of a central meeting point, modes of accompaniment, the composition and make-up of groups, temporal and spacial differences in time spent and routes followed, and post-pub and club events. While it is possible to make some overall generalisations, these patterns and routes are influenced by a range of factors deserving additional in-depth study.

Pre-night out activities includes planning the evening, getting dressed and ready, and in some cases 'warming up'. Nights out for locals were often carefully planned in advance and were made possible by an intricate set of telephone networks. Usually there was a key person to call to get the latest update on the evening itinerary. Students appeared to be somewhat more spontaneous in this regard, possibly due to the fact that they were more likely to be in daily contact with friends and house-mates whom they usually went out with. Similarly, while getting ready and dressed up was an important ritual for locals, which sometimes involved meeting beforehand at someone's house, students again appeared to be more relaxed and casual about this aspect. Prior to going out, the main pattern for students involved either a meal or simply a gathering at someone's house as a warm-up for the night ahead, and this often involved drinking and perhaps drug-taking. Due to their domestic situation of being more likely to be living at home, locals tended to go straight from home to a 'meeting' pub.

The majority of locals mentioned the importance of a central meeting point or a warm-up pub. The Monument, a tall statue in the city centre, is a well recognised meeting point as are pubs located near this area or near major bus stops. Meeting pubs tended to be away from areas one would eventually end up and in some cases acted as a point of contact for anyone in a group who had not arranged to meet beforehand. The average time locals met up was between 7-7:30 and the warm-up pub was one of the few places where more than one drink might be consumed. The average length of stay here was also longer and ranged between 45 minutes and an hour. 'Stop-off' pubs, or bars on route to where groups were headed were also popular and often one or two of these would be visited for a quick drink before arriving at a specific area of the city.

A typical although not exclusive pattern for locals was pub-crawling (see **Map 1 and taped extract**). From the meeting pub this basically involved a one drink stop of approximately 20 minutes at roughly 7-10 bars or pubs within easy walking distance. Often groups had rigorous schedules of being at a particular place at a specific time every week. This habitual pattern meant that the evening was largely pre-planned and it was possible for different groups to link up with one another through the night. 'Neck-ins', as some locals refer to them, also assured that a specific amount of alcohol was likely to be consumed, although it was possible to alter this by switching from say pints to halves. In many ways this pattern of going out drinking maximises the consumption of alcohol under the current licensing laws. Last orders just before 11:00 means the majority of people are leaving pubs and bars at around 11:30. Locals were more likely to spend money on taxis and food at the end of the night, usually a quick take-away, so many were actually home just after midnight.

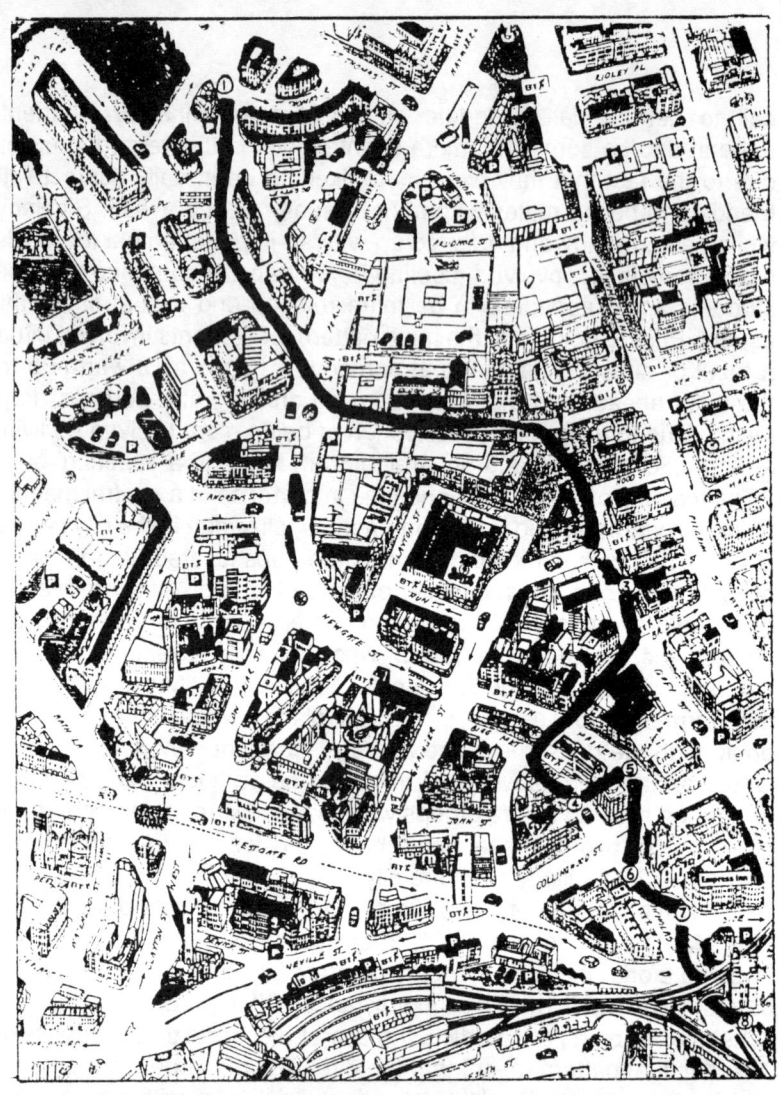

MAP 1- Route and Description of Local Night Out (Dan L26)

As I say, w' always meet in the Trent about half seven to eight o'clock. We always stay there for about an hour, maybe two or three drinks if w' stay in, so we leave there about quarter to nine. Say we gan' to the Bigg Market and probably gan' to Legends. Have one in there, er, come out of there about quarter past nine, twenty past nine, then to the Adelphi, have one in there. Leave there about half past nine,and to Maceys, say come out there about ten to ten, er, Balmbra's, come out of there about quarter past ten. Then to Masters, come out of there about twenty-five to eleven, then go to the Empress or the Bridge for last orders, come out of there and then sometimes go to the nightclub.

46

This local pattern, although popular, does not exhaust the wide range of Geordie nights out. A significant number of locals mentioned they had progressively moved away somewhat from the Bigg Market area and the pattern of going out associated with it. This 'branching out' involved, amongst other things, utilising other parts of the city such as the Quayside, Haymarket and Station areas and going to different types of pubs, including student ones, or instituting a regular club visit after a night out. Other locals restricted themselves solely to a particular type of pub which suited their lifestyle or cultural orientation and would stay there all evening. A sub-section of young locals into a particular dance and/ or music culture, adopted a pattern of going out more closely resembling that of students discussed next.

Overall students adopted a different pattern of going out when compared to locals, although pub-crawling was also engaged in. They tended to go out later, with a less fixed itinerary, although this may have to do with the fact that students are more apt to experiment by trying out a variety of places. On average, students tended to visit fewer places and stay longer (see **Map 2 and taped extract** for one example). It was not uncommon for groups to go out later and yet have the same amount of drinking time as locals due to extended union bar licenses. Students were also more likely to attend music venues and go on to clubs following pubs. A section of the university population who were heavily into the dance/ music scene would sometimes make their way straight from home to a club, or use a pub simply as a meeting point or warm up to clubbing. Students were also more likely to be involved in post-night out activities, again aided by their domestic situation, by having house parties following pub and sometimes club closures.

Patterns of accompaniment and the composition of groups on nights out also were influenced by differences between the local and student population as well as others factors. Overall, nights out tend to be a collective phenomenon and as we have mentioned the make-up and membership of these networks are very important. Nearly two-thirds of the sample went out in either a group (3-5) or a gang (over 5 people). At the same time going out involves wider interaction and socialising, and these gangs would sometimes link together and reform over the course of the night. This was true for both students and locals, with groups growing in numbers to 15 or 20 in some cases. Only 13% of the sample regularly went out with only one other person who was likely to be either a best friend or a partner, while the remainder had a more variable pattern.

47

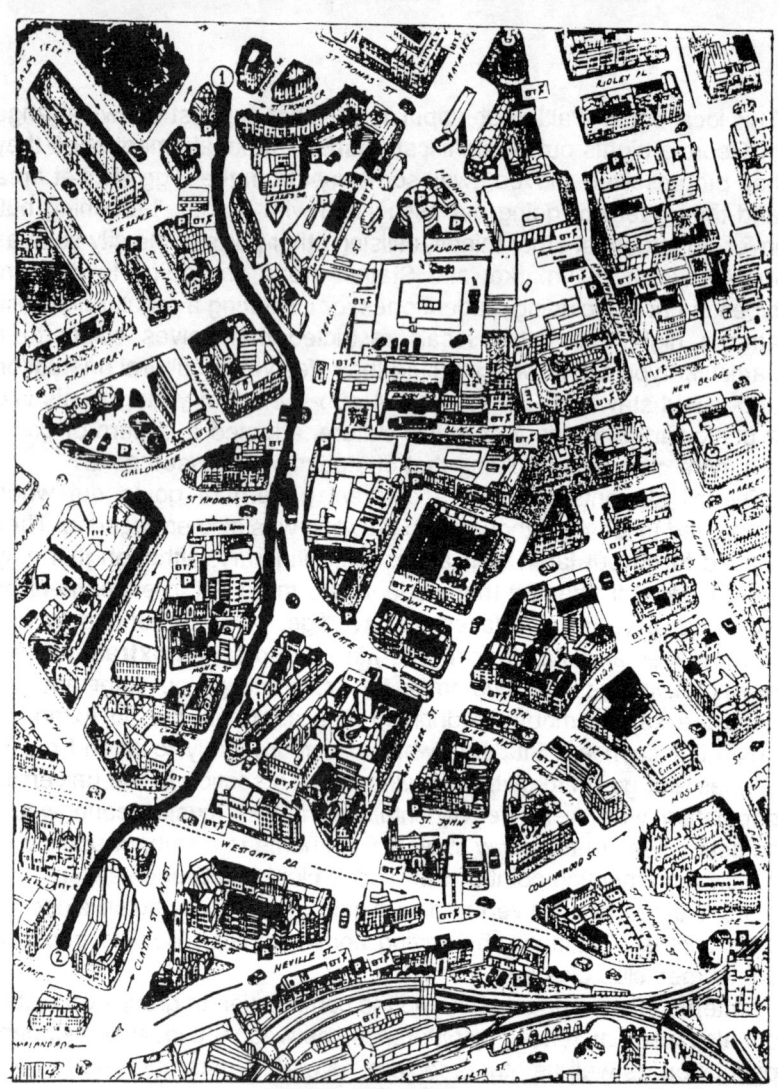

MAP 2- Route and Description of Student Night Out (Alice S22)

We usually go out about nine o'clockish or something like that. Oh, em, yea, we usually go out with the girls in my house, but if we are meeting anyone then we'll phone then up, we usually meet them, perhaps outside the Haymarket at a certain time, or in the Union at a certain time. But we'll get ready for about eight and then we'll have a few drinks downstairs. Then we'll go out, perhaps to the Union for a pint first, or the Trent House, em, then we'll go on to the club about ten, half past ten. We'll come out, perhaps we'll get a pizza or some chips and then get a taxi home. If there is a party going on, yea, we'll go up to it, but when you're living in like Jesmond it's a bit hard for us, so we don't go to as many as the people in Fenham do.

48

Local men were more apt to go out in gangs, while local women had a much more diverse pattern of accompaniment, which included all women gangs and groups, a female best friend or boyfriend. Over half of locals went out regularly in single sex groups (55% of women and 54% of men), one third went out in mixed groups, with the remainder having a varied pattern. Surprisingly, only 20% of the local sample knew the people they went out with through work, while double this percentage knew them through school, and one-third actually met members of their group on a night out. This demonstrates the importance of nights out over and above work as a basis for socialising.

The size of student groups and gangs tended to be related to the number of people in the household or the breadth of their circle of friends. Eighty percent went out in groups or gangs, with 77% knowing group members through the university and 40% being house or flatmates. Very few students went out with only one other person, and even couples tended to join in with a larger crowd. Student groups also tended to be more mixed, with over 60% saying that they regularly went out with both men and women, while only a third went out in single sex groups. Part of the rationale for large, mixed gatherings may have to do with issues of housing, for example large numbers of students linking up to return to their university accommodations, or safety. However, students did appear to be much more casual about whether groups were mixed or not, while locals seem to have a stronger tradition of separate lads and lasses nights out.

Drinking

In earlier sections we hinted at the role alcohol occupies in nightlife culture and the way in which drinking patterns have changed historically in an area like the North East. Here we want to concentrate primarily on conveying some basic information on the drinking habits of both our local and student cohorts. Part of the reason for doing so concerns a kind of mystique around the subject, but also to call into question some of the stereotypical beliefs particularly surrounding local drinking behaviours.

The centrality of alcohol as a key ritual in nights out is beyond question. Getting drunk was the third most popular reason young adults gave to explain the significance of going out. While there is some evidence that illegal drugs may be beginning to rival some of the functions of drinking, the consumption of alcohol continues to be the main activity engaged in. Ninety-eight percent of young adults in our sample drink alcohol when they go out, while only 2% abstained. The average age when young people had their first drink in a pub or club was 15.4 years old, with the majority developing a pattern of going out and having alcohol on average two and a half times per week.

The most popular drink consumed on nights out amongst our sample was beer. Eighty percent drank beer regularly, with students and local men being the main consumers. The next favourite category of drink was shorts, with nearly 50% of the sample drinking them regularly. This general category of drink was particularly popular amongst women, including students as well as locals. Cider and Castaway were also almost exclusively consumed by women, with wine, cocktails and snakebite (a mixture of cider and beer) being minority choices.

Additionally we gathered some further information on the type and brand name of drink consumed and the reasons why they were chosen. The stereotype that all young Geordie's drink only premium bottled lagers is at best only a half truth. While local women preferred lager on tap when they do drink beer, they are more likely to purchase a range of other alcoholic drinks. Strong ciders and sweet liqueurs like Baileys and Tia Maria were also popular as was the consumption of Castaway. While showing a preference for imported bottled lagers like Becks, Coors, Pils, Red Stripe and Budweiser, as lager on tap is considered to be too watered down, local men also displayed a wider taste for bitters, ales and stouts. Guinness was popular, particularly in the winter and when one had some extra cash, as was bitter (Theaksons) and Scotch. Contrary to public opinion, there are a number of Bigg Market pubs which do sell ales and stouts.

Student tastes appeared to be dictated by a conflict between what they liked and what they could afford. This is probably the main reason why beer remains the main student beverage. While they were more likely to favour real ales, stouts and premium imported lagers, financially they were more apt to buy whatever was the cheapest. Additionally, student's higher consumption of shorts and cocktails is also partly explained by the timing and prices of happy hours and student nights, which often included cheap drinks in city centre pubs and bars. Again, the price of liquor rather than brand names appeared to be the main factor determining purchases.

One of the most contentious issues surrounding young adults and alcohol are levels of consumption. Regional Trends (No 28, 1993) provides a rough definition of low, moderate and high consumption levels for both males and females (aged 16 or over), as well as giving regional comparisons. The North has the highest percentage of males (32%) in the high consumption category (22+ units of alcohol per week), while women rank third in this regard with 11% in the high category defined as 15+ units per week. One would reasonably expect that our sample of 16-31 year olds would surpass these overall consumption figures for the population as a whole.

Making sense of the consumption of alcohol is complicated by the different ways in which findings can be presented. **Figure 2** provides information on both the number of units consumed on an average night out, as well as an average weekly consumption figure for our sample.[12] The highest consumption figure for units of alcohol consumed on an average night out is local men, who drink on average 12.6 units (about 6.3 pints), followed closely by student men (11 units per night out or 5.5 pints). Local women narrowly out drink student women by consuming 7.8 units as opposed to student's 7.2. According to these overall figures there are not really major differences in the amounts consumed per evening between these groups. If however one extracts out a sub-group within the local population, which we have labelled Bigg Market 'regulars', the figures change in an interesting way for both males and females. Overall, this sub-group does consume more units in an average evening than either students or their local counterparts. Males in this group consumed 14.8 units on an average night (roughly 7.4 pints), while women consumed 9.5 units. However, the net effect of removing this sub-group from their respective population means that in effect, non-Bigg Market Geordies actually consume less alcohol per night than students. At the same time, while this more detailed analysis confirms that locals in the Bigg Market generally drink more on an evening, the difference may not seem quite as striking as the stereotype would suggest.

Figure 2 also reveals some interesting data concerning weekly consumption figures for locals and students. Differences in the frequency of going out leads to a reversal of the above findings. Student men consume on average 31.2 units of alcohol per week, while local men average only 29.6 units (even the Bigg Market regulars consume less units per week than male students). Both of these averages are well into the 'high' consumption category. Even more dramatic are the consumption levels of student women. Due to the frequency with which they go out student women completely overshadow local women by drinking 23.8 units per week, while the

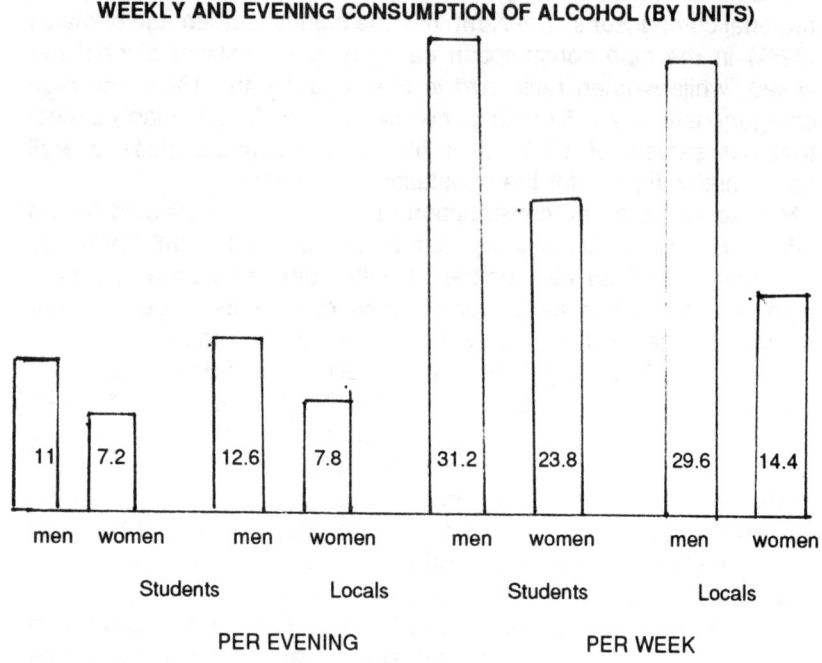

FIGURE TWO

WEEKLY AND EVENING CONSUMPTION OF ALCOHOL (BY UNITS)

| 11 | 7.2 | 12.6 | 7.8 | 31.2 | 23.8 | 29.6 | 14.4 |

| men | women | men | women | men | women | men | women |

| Students | Locals | Students | Locals |

| PER EVENING | PER WEEK |

latter group manage only 14.4 units. Again according to recommended levels, local women fall into the 'moderate' category, while student women are excessively above the 'high' consumption standard (15+ units per week).

These latter figures suggest that there may be somewhat of an inverse relationship between the long term health risks associated with high weekly consumption patterns and the significance the public attributes to various social problems created through bouts of over-indulgence. In this regard, we also asked our sample a range of questions on problems they experienced through drinking on nights out. They were vomiting or being sick, passing out, getting into an argument or fight, unable to get up in the morning and losing days from work. While the majority of people who consume alcohol have probably experienced all or some of these symptoms sometime in their lives, we were particularly concerned to discover persistent difficulties.

The main overall finding was that the vast majority of our sample did not report regular problems with respect to drinking. Between 90 and 100% stated that they did not suffer any of the symptoms listed above 'on a regular basis'. The most common problem experienced by our sample was getting up in the morning after drinking, with 12% stating that this was a common occurrence. Nearly 10% also stated they regularly lost days from work or education through the after effects of drink. While there is a range of literature suggesting that there is an economic as well as a health concern about working time lost, the above figures were in fact substantially inflated by our student cohort (17% had problems getting up in the morning and the same percentage admitted missing classes frequently due to over-indulgence). A further 10% of the sample said that drinking regularly led to arguments, yet for the most part these disagreements were largely between friends and were viewed as trivial and non-confrontational. A minority (5%) stated that they were often sick through drink and only 1.5% said they passed out regularly.

Overall, it did not appear that the majority of young adults perceived drinking as either a personal or social problem, and perhaps this partly helps to explain the continued popularity of this past-time on nights out. Alcohol does play an important socialising role in our society and if used sensibly it can enhance, rather than diminish social interaction. This is not to say however that alcohol should be privileged in this regard or is without problems. However, rather than focus on minority incidents involving anti-social behaviour caused through excess drinking, we should perhaps start to concentrate more on longer term health issues concerning weekly consumption figures.

Drugs

The ongoing debate about the prevalence of illegal drug use, its social implications and legal status is a complex and convoluted one. The issue of youth and drugs is often complicated by public misinformation and media hysteria and a failure to distinguish between types of drugs used, patterns of use and the socio-cultural dimensions of drug-taking. Furthermore, much of the public debate about drugs takes place in the absence of any contribution from those people who actually use and have knowledge of them (Coffield and Gofton, 1994). Here we rely primarily on our own sample to highlight their views and experiences of illegal drug taking.

Two-thirds of our sample reported that they had taken drugs on, before or following a night out. The most popular drug consumed was cannabis, with 63% saying they had used it in conjunction with going out. Thirty percent had taken speed/ amphetamines, 18% had taken acid and ecstasy and 7% had tried cocaine. Three percent had taken LSD and only 2% had ever tried heroin and magic mushrooms.

It is crucial to put these seemingly high consumption figures into context. Clearly the only drug taken by the majority of our sample was cannabis and it is no surprise to find that the main debate around legalisation and decriminalisation centred around this substance. The majority of young people, even non-users, were largely positive about cannabis in terms of its cost, its relatively low health risks and 'after effects' and the drugs 'sociability factor':

Ade (S23)   *I think cannabis should be legalised, I think alcohol is far more harmful. And I think you know it doesn't create fights, it does create people getting angry, it has a lot of benefits to people who suffer from certain diseases. I think putting up the fine recently is stupid.*

Kate (L22)   *I don't agree with drugs, they are just bad news. But I think cannabis should be legalised because of what I've researched about it. It doesn't seem to do you any more harm than tobacco, so I can't really understand why its illegal.*

It is also important to note that while over sixty percent had taken cannabis on, before or following a night out, the majority were not regular users. Most smoked it only when it was available from friends or house-mates and only a minority actually bought and used it regularly.

Early media reports about the prevalence of ecstasy also appear to be somewhat exaggerated by our findings. Part of the reason may be due to the fact that it became well known through the local drug grapevine that the supply of ecstasy had diminished in quality, not to mention concern over a number of recent deaths and its long-term effects. Ecstasy or 'E' use however was closely tied to the 'rave' or post-rave scene (Merchant and MacDonald, 1994), engaged in by elements of the student and local population and was clearly still prevalent in these circles:

Ellen(S21)   *I don't actually take E's which is quite rare, cos all*
                  my friends do. They all take like chemical drugs.

Acid was as popular as ecstasy and speed even more so, suggesting
that young adults are experimenting with a range of substances rather
than limiting themselves solely to a particular drug consumption style.
This raises the important issue and effect of multiple or 'poly' drug
use.

The type of use young adults make of this middle-band of illegal
drugs is also important for putting into context public misconceptions.
For example, popular notions of getting 'hooked' on drugs, or climbing
the 'drug ladder', completely ignores that different drugs have different
levels and categories of dependency, for example physical as opposed
to psychological. The fact is that the majority of young people are
either 'recreational/ weekend' or 'experimental' users. Only 3% of our
sample described their use of drugs as problematic and both were
completely drug-free at the time they were interviewed. As our
statistics show, heroin use was virtually non-existent and there
appeared to be little evidence of crack use.

Taking these experiences into account it is not surprising to find that
the majority of young adults we interviewed were in favour of the
legalisation of some drugs. Seventy-four percent felt that some drugs
should be legalised, 18% were unsure, with only 8% against. Students
were more likely to favour legalisation than locals. Of those in favour,
86% mentioned that cannabis should be legalised, with 14% saying all
illegal drugs should be made available. The main reasons given were
the lifting of criminal prosecution, to ensure the purity of substances,
and reduce problems with dealing. There was also an expressed
desire amongst a section of the sample to provide night-time facilities
conducive to smoking cannabis, similar to the Dutch cafe system.

Sex and courtship

With the exception of drink, sex is probably the most talked about
aspect of going out. There are a number of reasons for this, some of
which have already been mentioned. The recognition that the
courtship function of going out (meeting someone, dating, getting

married) has become undermined by rapid social, cultural and economic change has meant that sexual relations have increasingly become separated out from this historic process. Some young adults viewed this separation of sex from courtship as not only possible, but desirable. This idea is supported by the fact that nearly one in five of our sample said meeting a sexual partner was one of the main reasons for having nights out. While this subgroup tended to be local, male, younger and usually single, there has also been a change in the attitudes of many young women in relation to sexual matters. While there is a strong public perception that the pursuit of sexual relations is indeed the only reason why young adults now go out, our findings suggest that continuities with courtship do exist and there is often a disjuncture between attitudes and actual behaviour.

The interesting thing about sex in our society is how much time and energy we put into talking about it, in relation to actually doing it. Surveys of sexual behaviour show that the average number of sexual partners is inflated by the fact that a minority of people are very sexually active, while the majority are far less so. A Wellcome Trust sponsored survey of 19,000 people in England, Wales and Scotland, found that 46% of men and 60% women aged 16-24 reported having only one sexual partner over the last year, while only 3.5% and 1% respectively had more than five (The Guardian 3.12.92). Due to the unrealistic expectations our society holds about meeting a sexual partner on a night out, the difference between talk and reality may be even wider.

We asked our sample whether they felt that the discussion about sex on nights out was exaggerated, or whether it was likely to happen more frequently. While over half said that sex happened more frequently on nights out, over 40% felt that it was exaggerated talk. The main reason given by the former group was they had either witnessed it frequently or heard about sexual conquests from friends, while the latter group tended to utilise their own experience in justifying the statement that the incidence of sex was blown out of proportion. Interestingly enough, men were more apt to say that such talk was exaggerated, while women were more likely to say that they thought sex occurred frequently on nights out.

We also asked our sample about their own sexual behaviour on nights out. The average number of sexual partners met 'specifically on a night out' over the last year was 1.5 per person. Men (both locals and students) appeared to be the most sexually active with 1.7 partners met on a night out over the last year. Student women averaged 1.5 sexual partners and local women were the least sexually active with 1.2 partners. Yet even these surprisingly low figures actually inflate the activity levels of the average night-time reveller. For example, 10% of the sample accounts for 63% of the total number of sexual contacts. In other words, there is a small number of very sexually active young adults, and a large majority who have a low activity level. If we remove this active group from the overall total, the average number of sexual partners met on a night out over the last year drops to less than one (0.6) per person.

This low activity level was confirmed by further data collected on whether or not our sample had 'ever' developed a relationship with someone on a night out, and what the status of that relationship was. Only 38% stated they had ever had a one night stand following a night out. While locals were marginally more likely than students to have a one night stand, they were also on average older and had been going out longer. In fact, all young adults were twice as likely to develop a long-term or dating relationship with someone they met, than to have a one night stand. A significant number mentioned that they had met their current partner on a night out. Going out for the majority then appears to be much more closely associated with the traditional pattern of meeting someone and dating, than it does with catching someone's eye across the bar and ending up in bed with them that evening.

Despite the fact that young adults in our sample do not appear to be very sexually active on nights out, the issue of sexual health with respect to HIV/ AIDS remains an important one. This is particularly the case for the 10% who are highly active and have multiple sexual partners, but it also has implications for the educational and awareness levels of young adults generally. We asked our sample whether or not HIV/ AIDS had changed their idea of what constitutes a good night out. While one-third of them said it had, just over half stated that it had not affected their idea of a good night out. These figures reflect similar trends found in a Health Education Authority survey of 8000 young people which found that although condom use had increased, two-thirds of the sample saw no need to change their lifestyle because of AIDS (The Guardian 7.12.90).

Responding in either the affirmative or negative however was not a guarantee that young people were enlightened about the facts concerning HIV/ AIDS. For example, one women who said it had affected her idea of a good night out, simply said that she was more careful as to the 'type' of person she slept with, as if someone with the virus could be easily spotted. Another respondent said he felt AIDS explained why an increased number of young adults were turning to other pursuits like dance, music or drinking as the main focus of their night out. Some of those who said it had not affected their nights out cited their use of condoms, abstinence, or allegiance to their partner as their rationale, while others suggested that the chance of contracting the virus was so slim they preferred not to worry.

To conclude, it is important to reiterate the yawning gap between public perceptions of the relationship between promiscuity and nights out and the actual reality of sexual contact. This is not to argue that sex does not happen or that sexuality is unimportant. On the contrary, symbolically it is probably one of the most central components of going out. However, much of the investment made here is displaced into clothing, posture, interaction, innuendo and conversation. Young women, in particular are increasingly taking control of their own sexuality- partly by asserting themselves as equal partners but also by constructing contradictory images of themselves as sexual beings (i.e. the controversial 'school girl' look). Young men continue to assert their masculine identity through control of the body (i.e. body building), verbal affirmations of sexual conquests and sometimes through sexual aggression and violence. Other fragments of the youth population struggle with notions of the 'new man' and 'post-feminism', while still others turn towards the more androgenous community of various music and dance cultures. Finally, while the spectre of AIDS has not yet resulted in sexual enlightenment amongst young adults, it has certainly cast a shadow of doubt and insecurity on this important aspect of social life.

Music/ dancing

The centrality of music to youth culture has been well recognised (Frith, 1978). More recently, the combination of dance, music and drug cultures have received considerable attention both academically and in the popular press. In terms of our research findings, it is significant to note that dance/ music was more likely to be cited as one of the main reasons why young people went on nights out than meeting a sexual partner and 80% of our sample spent money going to clubs. Furthermore, the same percentage said that the type of music played influenced where they went and over 60% said dancing played an important part in their night out.

We asked our respondents to indicate their preference with regard to three forms of musical presentation- live music, disc jockey (DJ) and background. Overall, the most popular choice was a DJ (38%), followed closely by background (31%) and surprising live music (31%). The popularity of DJs mirrors economic trends in both the type and technological presentation of contemporary music, although it should be noted that there is a commercial as well as an alternative scene here. A number of young adults were extremely conversant with the work of particular DJs, to the extent that they would follow individuals from club to club or city to city. The main reason for preferring DJ'ed music appeared to be not only the quality of the music, but visual presentation and the innovative way that the music was put together.

Background music was also popular and important in terms of where pub goers went on nights out. Many suggested they simply would not go to places which did not play their brand of music and a number of establishments were renowned for the quality of their 'jukebox'. Some pubs specialised in soul, R&B or indie music and attracted specific audiences. Other respondents went to pubs for other reasons, to talk or socialise, and as long as the background music was not too loud or annoying, it was seen as relatively unimportant.

Live music as a preference matched background music, with nearly one third of the sample giving it as their first choice. This may be somewhat of a surprise considering previous research which suggests that Tyneside has historically been on the periphery in terms of producing home grown talent, attracting established bands into the area and cultivating a live music culture (Wilkinson and Cornford, 1990). Additionally, our own findings showed that only about 5-8% of nights out were specifically to see a live band. However, the formation of 'Generator', a collective of music promoters, managers and artists in the region, and the development of venues like the Riverside, has meant that live music is beginning to make some important strides forward in the city.

By breaking our sample down, one can get a clearer picture of some general differences in musical preference within the subgroups. Background music was most popular amongst the local population, with a general predilection for the latest chart hits. This however, was followed closely by DJs, with live music the least popular (still nearly a quarter chose this). Students, on the other hand, were more likely to chose DJ, followed closely by live music. They were also much more likely than locals to say the type of music influenced where they went on a night out (96% as compared to 60%).

While obviously connected, dancing played a slightly less significant role than music in most people's night out, partly because of the increased personal investment the former activity implies. An additional problem is the 'no dancing' policy of many establishments in the city centre. However, over 60% of the sample said it was an important part of their night out and there was a smaller but highly dedicated club clientele within this group. Again, students were twice as likely than locals to say that dancing played a significant part in their night out, with local men being the group least likely to say this. This overall pattern was contradicted by a small number of younger Geordie men who were heavily into the local dance and music scene.

Although the research was not designed to examine musical styles and cultures in detail, a number of field visits to different venues around the city were made. Clearly, there has been an explosion in the variety of music, specialist club nights and atmosphere in many of Newcastle's clubs and music venues, with many styles being catered for. The Riverside, in particular, has been a driving force since it opened its doors in 1985 and its recent expansion means that two separate venues can be put on at the same time. It puts on an average of three live bands a week, playing a wide variety of music, and has more recently began to experiment with specialist dance club nights. Other clubs have followed suit and play a variety of specialist music which include 60s and 70s nights, house, garage, jungle, techno, reggae, acid jazz, funk, rock, and indie amongst others (the Riverside's monthly venue 'Bloated' is advertised as 'alternative guitar based noise').

Perhaps the single largest music and dance based phenomenon of the late 1980s and early nighties was rave culture (Redhead, 1993; Merchant and MacDonald, 1994). Newcombe (1991, p 4) defines a rave somewhat stiffly as 'a long period of constant energetic and stylistic dancing exhibited by a large group of people in a hot, crowded facility providing continuous loud House music and an accompanying strobe-lit psychedelic light show'. From the early illegal days of 'Acid House' and the designer drug ecstasy, rave, if it can even be said to exist any more, has become much more diversified as well as commercial in orientation. Many clubs in the city, not to mention student unions, provide a commercial version of rave music, albeit in its different forms (ambient, techno, garage, hardcore, jungle etc).

One individual's recollection of a rave night in the city reinforces one academic finding concerning this culture, the phenomenon of cross-class participation:

Rob (S23)   *That stage of rave would be blanked out as being sort of white all in one sort of outfits and then you get in [to the venue] and its running around with tops off. You get these big Geordies, you normally wouldn't expect to speak to in the street, because they'd be quite anti-student, and you'd just be there and you'd be sort of hugging them, shaking their hands.*

While there were a small number of respondents in our sample who were seriously into rave culture at one stage, its incorporation into the mainstream has meant that many either reject the label or have become further immersed into a particular variation of the music.

Surprisingly, with all this differentiation in terms of provision, one of our samples main criticism of Newcastle's nightlife was a lack of variety in the club scene. While this is changing, it would appear that the insatiable quest for new and different musical and dance styles continuously outstrips the provision of existing venues. Further research into specific music cultures and audiences is a never ending process and more research into this area is solely needed.

Violence, disorder and vandalism

Cities have a long history of association with crime and disorder. This combined with the twin ingredients of young people and alcohol further fuels images of violence and danger. While not wanting to completely discount the possibility that these combination of factors can indeed produce serious acts of anti-social behaviour, our research findings attempt to put into context the amount of disorder that goes on, where it occurs, and looks at young people's own views and experiences of this phenomenon. We also look at the issue of sexual harassment on nights out as a form of violence against women. In doing so we rely primarily on four types of data- national crime statistics and reports (for comparative purposes), local police records, independent research conducted on incidents recorded by the city's CCTV cameras and most importantly, young adults own experiences and recollections of violence, vandalism and harassment.

Available national statistics do show there are higher crime rates in metropolitan as opposed to non-metropolitan areas (Social Trends 22, HMSO 1992, p. 17) and higher rates generally in mixed inner metropolitan areas as opposed to affluent suburbs (The British Crime Survey 1992, reported in The Guardian 27.10.92). However, there may be a number of reasons why this may be so and one also needs to be careful to distinguish between crimes of property and crimes against the person. Additionally one should not automatically assume that violent crime is limited to 'deprived' cities. In 1987 there were more than 250 'riots' which occurred in rural locations (The Guardian 10.6.88), and a Home Office study on disorder in non-metropolitan areas demonstrated that a significant proportion of rural disturbances revolve around drinking and pub going by reasonably affluent young people (HMSO, 1989).

Local statistics obtained from Northumbria police by sub-division from 1991-3 and a Home Office study of disorder in Newcastle conducted a decade ago (Hope, 1983), initially appear to show that violence is more prevalent in the city centre and that there is a link between the incidence of assaults and their proximity to pubs and clubs. Of the five police sub-divisions, a disproportionate percentage of assaults and wounding, drunkenness and public order offenses do occur in Newcastle centre. Yet even these bare statistics need to be put into some kind of context. For instance, there is clearly a much higher density of people visiting the city centre in the evenings, with it being estimated that Newcastle attracts some 15,000 young adults on a busy Friday night. With its 151 pubs there is also a much higher percentage of individuals drinking in this area, and detection rates may be higher due to a much more pervasive police presence there. It is also important to note that assaults and wounding in the city centre only account for approximately 3% of all recorded crime committed there, drunkenness 14%, public order offenses 5% and drugs less than 1%. Figures for the last two years (1992-3) show that of the 15 murders in 5 police areas, only 2 occurred in the city centre.[13]

Without playing down the seriousness of this issue, our survey results reveal that young people have quite a different experience of levels of violence and vandalism on nights out than one might expect. We asked our sample not only whether they felt the city and areas of the city were dangerous, but also to recall the number of violent incidents and examples of vandalism that they both witnessed and were personally involved in over the entire period of time they had been going out. It was then possible to divide the number of incidents by the number of visits made, to come up with a 'danger quotient'.[14]

The main finding concerning young adult's perceptions of violence is that 82% actually felt that the danger element was exaggerated with respect to the areas they used in nights out. This was generally the case for both locals and students and was perhaps most emphatically felt by some of those utilising the Bigg Market area of the city. While just over half of the sample thought there were 'trouble-spots', most admitted that their ideas where based largely on hearsay rather than experience. The vast majority were prone to refer to the Bigg Market in this regard, although the Green Market area at the bottom of Eldon Square was also mentioned, with locals being as likely as students to mention these areas. However, forty percent of the entire sample felt that there were no real danger areas in Newcastle city centre, suggesting that the threat of violence is viewed as far less of a problem for those who actually use this space than it is for the general public. This perhaps helps to explain the apparent paradox of why young adults continue to use the city centre for nights out, despite media hype about its dangers.

Seventy-seven percent of the sample had never been personally involved in a fight or a violent incident. The 23% who had been involved recalled a total of 23 incidents or 1.6 fights per person over the entire time they had been going out, with the highest single number of altercations for one person being four. While locals were more likely than students to be involved, the difference was not dramatic (30% as compared to 17%), and surprisingly local women were the group with the highest percentage experiencing an act of personal violence (40%). Bigg Market regulars were in fact slightly less likely to be involved in a fight, although they made up a disproportionate percentage of the total number of incidents (i.e. a few regulars had a high number of altercations). However, these local and perhaps gender figures were skewed not by the 'Bigg Market effect', but by a small number of individuals, including women, who had made many visits to the city centre over an extended period of time and had a pattern of patronising particularly 'rough' places at one stage of their drinking career. A number of these incidents involved bouncers, gangs of male youths or conflicts between football supporters.

A more telling statistic can be obtained by dividing the number of incidents by the total number of nights out. Using this calculation, the chances of getting involved personally in a fight was once every 970 nights out. This finding, not to mention the figures above, are consistent with a larger study conducted on violence in the pub (Marsh, 1980). Based on going out two times per week, an individual would experience, on average, one violent altercation approximately every 9.5 years. The ratio for students was even more remote, one fight for every 1416 visits, while locals could expect personal involvement once every 805 nights out. Due to the involvement of a small number of Bigg Market regulars in a high number of incidents, as a whole this group's chances of being involved personally in a fight were higher with one incident every 400 visits, yet even here this meant about only one altercation every 5 years.

From these overall figures it is clear to see that the vast majority of young adults have never been personally involved in a fight and the remainder had in fact only suffered one or two incidents on average over the entire time they have been going out. Overall, the chances of being in an violent altercation appears to be extremely small when compared with the vast number of times people visit the city centre in the evening. A small minority appear to seek out or attract trouble, either explicitly or perhaps inadvertently, through their behaviour or choice of pub/ bar and an even smaller percentage are unlucky victims.

The witnessing of violent incidents or fights was more common and it is this aspect, including the severity of some acts, that helps to explain general concerns over violence in city centres. Over three-quarters of our sample had witnessed a fight or violent altercation on a night out. Surprisingly perhaps, a higher percentage of students were more likely to report this than locals (80% as opposed to 73%). However, even when one takes into account the higher number of visits locals have made to the city centre, Geordies were still more apt to recall a much higher number of violent incidents- 20 on average per person, while students recalled only 3 per person. Again, these figures were skewed by a small number of individuals who had witnessed a large number of fights. Taken as a proportion of the total number of times our sample had gone out, the average person would witness one fight for every 32 visits made or, on the basis of two visits per week, they would probably see one incident every 4 months.

Due to the higher number of incidents recalled, locals were more apt to see fights more frequently- one incident for every 23 visits made. While one might hastily conclude that this increased frequency for Geordies is due to the 'Bigg Market effect', in fact people regularly using this area of the city actually reported witnessing slight less incidents per visit than non-Bigg Market locals (one fight per 22.6 visits made). This view is supported by a six month study of incidents recorded by the CCTV cameras, which appear to suggest that violence is not any more prevalent in the Bigg Market/ Groat Market area than the city as a whole (Centre for Research on Crime, Policing and the Community, 1993). In fact a further breakdown of these figures showed that the cameras located in this area recorded only 15 fights over a six month period in this area from April-Sept 1993. It also became clear, when we asked people to recount details of where violence had occurred, they were in fact spread throughout the city centre and tended to occur more frequently outside clubs and around taxi-ranks, buses and Metro Stations, as opposed to centring around any one area.

Involvement in and witnessing acts of vandalism appear to be even more remote and infrequent than fights. Only 13% admitted to ever personally being involved in any kind of vandalism, the vast majority of acts being petty in nature. Students were more likely to admit vandalism (17%) than locals (10%), with the major activities being traditional pranks such as stealing signs and traffic cones. Only half of our sample had ever witnessed acts of vandalism on a night out, with students again more apt to see this than locals (57% for students and only 43% for locals). However, locals tended overall to see a much higher number of acts of vandalism, even though again a significant number of them were recalled by a minority group of people. Locals reported seeing an act of vandalism on a night out once every 19 visits to the city centre, while students had to go out over 70 times to observe such an activity.

Finally, we looked at the issue of sexual harassment as a form of violence on nights out. Harassment can range from uninvited groping to verbal abuse and sexual innuendo and as McKinnon (1989) has argued 90% of women can expect it in some form during their lives. Sixty percent of our sample of women reported to have been sexually harassed on a night out, with half of the female respondents reporting actual physical contact. Local women were more likely than student women to suffer harassment with 73% as opposed to 47% reporting this. While reactions varied from shock to simply ignoring it, the vast majority of local women appeared to deal directly with this behaviour:

RT   *Have you experienced sexual harassment on a night out?*

Min (L27)   *Oh, not in Newcastle I don't think, except just like hassle from drunken bastards, maybe you know like, sort of feel you up something, but never like seriously.*

65

RT   *So how do you react to that?*

Min   *It would depend what kind of person they are, but
             usually I tell them to fuck off.*

While student women appeared less likely to suffer from sexual harassment on nights out there should be no room for complacency. A study at Oxford Brookes University showed that 7% of female students had been a victim of either rape, assault or indecent exposure while at the institution (The Guardian 20.12.94).

One of the main problems with looking at sexual harassment with respect to nights out in the city centre is that it diverts attention away from other areas of life where it may be equally prevalent and assumes that perpetrators are somehow 'out there' waiting in the streets. It may be as likely to occur in employment or education, in the community or in the family home, and the harasser more than likely may be known to the victim. In the university study quoted earlier, 91% of the rape cases happened at a place of residence and in 89% of the cases the offender was known to the victim. However, it is clear that while women construct various ways of dealing with the issue of sexual harassment, it can seriously curtail their involvement in and enjoyment of nights out.

In conclusion, we have sought to investigate and put into context much of the hyperbole about violence and vandalism on nights out. This is not to say that such acts never occur or that there are sometimes very serious and indeed devastating consequences. However, based on a wide range of existing data, including the experiences and perceptions of young adults themselves, we would have to conclude that personal involvement in violence is a relatively rare phenomenon on nights out. The vast majority of people can and do avoid potentially dangerous situations when they arise and mindless violence directed towards innocent victims, although unacceptable, is unusually rare. On the other hand, sexual harassment, although much more prevalent for at least a significant section of the population, has not received a similar amount of attention and concern.

There is a crying need for researchers in the 1990s, to turn again to more theoretically informed investigations of youth (sub) cultures which is cognizant of weaknesses and strengths in earlier traditions (MacDonald, Banks and Hollands, 1993)

5. Case Studies

One of the main arguments put forward in this book is that rapid economic, social and cultural change has resulted in an increased differentiation of youth adult's identities in the contemporary period. While the sample has been discussed primarily in terms of two main cohorts- locals and students- we have intimated that more specific youth cultural groupings exist. The recognition of these more distinctive and specific identities which cohere around particular activities, commodities, styles, focal concerns and territorial spaces, refers to a phenomenon known in the social sciences as 'youth sub-cultures', or perhaps more correctly, 'youth cultural identifications'.[15]

The case studies which follow introduce and examine some of these more specific youth responses in relation to the city. In doing so we are aware that there is neither the time or the space to even begin to analyze even a fraction of these contemporary cultural identifications in sufficient detail. What we would argue however is that the study of contemporary youth cultures is, after a twenty year lull, back on the agenda and that there is an extremely rich field of enquiry here. In selecting the following examples, we are explicitly calling for the revival of a type of cultural analysis which avoids some of the shortcomings of previous theoretical approaches, but which does not jettison some of the important elements of an economic and class-based analysis. Indeed, we begin by looking at a case study in which economic restructuring and the changing experience of class is at the very heart of the matter. We then go on to analyze student identities in relation to the city, before moving on to two examples of 'alternative' cultures- a new age pub and gay and lesbian spaces- as well as examine the phenomenon of 'ladies only' nights out.

The 'Bigg' Market...and beyond

When this research project was initially reported on by the media, and billed incorrectly as 'The Bigg Market research', what was most telling was the level of interest in and array of public images surrounding this area of the city. The Daily Express (August 28, 1993) described it as one of the 'nation's rowdiest watering holes' which had a reputation of 'drink-fuelled violence'.[16] Local responses to the project were also steeped in assumptions about the Bigg Market being the centre of wild, promiscuous and anti-social behaviour, and the supposedly common sense nature of the research in trying to explain the attraction of this area with regard to nights out. While the research was concerned with calling into question the accuracy of its reputation, the primary importance of the Bigg Market as a case study relates to its significance as a crucial site of local identity formation for young adults living in a region undergoing rapid economic change.

The Bigg Market, as a public space, has long been an arena of lively activity and this has no doubt helped to heighten its less than favourable reputation. It derived its name from a type of barley sold there and was the site of numerous busy markets, inns and hostelries in the 18th century. The Turk's Head Inn was well known for cock-fighting and the White Hart (in the Cloth Market) was a fashionable tavern which was particularly busy during race week and the commencement of the hunting season (Charlton, 1894). Curiously enough these places and activities were largely frequented by and undertaken by the upper classes.

The areas reputation as a centre for drinking and sociability continued into the 19th century and was extended to the working classes, represented by Lancaster's (1992, p. 59) assertion that most people failed to heed the middle class temperance campaigners Bigg Market drinking fountain caption of 'Water is Best'. In the course of conducting this research numerous older people mentioned the area as a site of activity throughout the 20th century, particularly around festivities such as New Years. Many of the taverns and pubs remained 'locals' catering primarily for male members of the working class into the 1960s.

The transformation of the Bigg Market into its contemporary form, occurred in the late 1970s and early 80s. A well known local entrepreneur, Joe Robertson, initially bought Pumphreys coffee shop in 1977 and turned it into a wine bar/ bistro type establishment. In a BBC2 programme ('Up North- The Bigg Market' 24.2.88), he perceptively identified a changing clientele and culture of drinking in the North East and outlined his role in providing more 'up-market' and salubrious city centre pubs/ clubs for young adults with relatively high disposable incomes. Robertson went on to buy up and transform over 27 bars and clubs in the city centre, many in the Bigg Market area, reselling most of them to a brewery chain and a leisure group in two main phases in 1984 and 1987.

The re-creation of the Bigg Market transformed the experience of going out and drinking in the city centre in a number of important ways. First, the up-market mixing of a pub/club atmosphere appealed to young working class Geordies who flocked to this area of the city. This was specifically the case for young local women, who had previously found themselves in a minority and un-catered for in many Newcastle city centre pubs and bars. As one thirty-eight year old women we interviewed in the pilot stage of this research stated 'I mean twenty years ago, apart from about three bars, they were men's bars in town'. Second, these developments began to change dress and drinking codes significantly, with the onset of circuit drinking and the familiar pattern of 'dressing up' to go out in Newcastle. Third, by the early 80s, a Home Office funded report was suggesting that levels of violence in the Bigg Market had begun to decline since the area was smartened up (Hope, 1983).

The real significance of the Bigg Market with respect to this study is not then so much its somewhat dated reputation as a 'problem area', although this issue does need to be addressed, but rather its colourful expression of one of the main themes of this book- young adult's identity formation in the context of economic and social change. It is more than coincidence that urban regeneration, in terms of the redevelopment of city centre pubs and clubs, occurred at precisely the same time as the region was experiencing its most rapid economic decline. While deindustrialization, particularly in the early 1980s, shook local communities and blocked young adult's movement into traditional work, opportunities for the expression of identity with respect to consumption in the city increased during this period. The importance of the Bigg Market for many young adults, relates to the fact that it is an important site for the modern expression of what it means to be a working class Geordie in a post-industrial climate.

The symbolic importance of the Bigg Market as a marker of contemporary regional identity, has meant that this area, and all it stands for, is both a source of fascination as well as a depository of public criticism. As the areas reputation as a nightspot grew nationally and even internationally, it came under scrutiny from both traditionalists and modernisers and became an easy scapegoat for all that was wrong in the region. On the one hand, nights out in the area

COMMENTS ON THE BIGG MARKET

Kevin (L25)   *It's like when I say to people like, we've been down the town on a Friday night, they say, who've you been with, then you go through what the people that you go out with do, and you've got the likes of people like Bob and Stan that are lecturers, there's me, there's a labourer, there's... you know. They think it's all like sort of Geordie boys, unemployed, who just go out to kick somebody's head in on a weekend kind of thing. And I don't see where they're getting it from me, cos people always say to me, you know, why do you go down the Bigg Market, cos it's rough, and it's not, it's just sort of just made up, and people are, it's just like a reputation that it's had years ago.*

Viv (L25)   *The Bigg Market I hate, because its so expensive, it is loud, rude, it is vulgar. Everything I don't want in a night out is there.*

Art (S26)   *I'd probably say [his best night out] the first time I went out in Newcastle, into the Bigg Market. I didn't feel threatened in any way, just that it was complete culture shock. Just seeing the amount of people out and seeing some of things that went on. We tend to have some fairly good conversations with some of the local Geordie blokes and you also tend to have a laugh with some of the older Geordie women. And they tend to be taking the mick most of the time, but its all good humoured...give you their handbag to look after and stuff.*

Leeanne (L19)   *Well the Bigg Market has got the you know, like the reputation...Well put it this way, all the times I've been there I've never seen a fight yet.*

Ade (S23)   *I probably wouldn't go to the Bigg Market. That's not really my scene and I don't get the impression that students are that welcome there.*

Joyce (S21)   *Em, I think it's a good atmosphere, em, cos I go, I've been to other places, and you just look around and people look like they're bored stupid or whatever, but I think what attracts us to the Bigg Market is the fact that there is always like quite loud music on and everybody is laughing and I mean, and you can be sitting in the toilet and there's loads of girls giggling and laughing and I don't know, we just have a good laugh and I think you just get involved in it cos it's a good atmosphere.*

70

were viewed by some as representing the more course and vulgar elements of an industrial working class in terminal decline, while others saw the new up market culture as commercially excessive and an affront to traditional local community values. As such, the Bigg Market came to represent and symbolise all that was bad about the night time economy- commercially crass pubs masquerading as clubs playing loud chart music, underage and excessive drinking, promiscuous and often violent behaviour. Hidden behind these negative images however was a broader context in which traditional identities, although blocked in some spheres, were being played out and even positively celebrated in the contemporary setting of the city.

Rather than understand the Bigg Market phenomenon in terms of these negative images and stereotypes, we would argue it is an illustrative case study of post adolescence and the ritualization of local identity. Rituals are a form of symbolic posturing, a reaffirmation of identity and culture. Lancaster (1992) has gone as far as utilising the notion of 'carnival' with respect to contextualising and understanding activities in the Bigg Market. The reconstruction of being a local by virtue of having a particular kind night out symbolises or stands in for a particular 'way of life' that is no longer possible. If young adults can never be a Geordie in a true occupational sense, the reconstruction of elements of such an identity can be derived from an imagined past and recast into a present persona. In essence, such a reconstruction can never be an authentic replica from the past, but rather borrows selectively on historical images and mixes these with a myriad of present day social circumstances and cultural experiences.

Masculine examples of this socially constructed local culture are evident in the Bigg Market and may take particular elements of this occupational history and exaggerate their form in the guise of the 'hard lads.' One respondent commented on the continued commemoration of the 'working man's weekend', despite the fact that far less young men are in employment and even fewer engage in manual work:

Geoff(L21)   *One of my friends calls it the 'working man's weekend', which is where you go out on a Friday night with the lads, and on a Saturday you go out with your girlfriend for a meal or something. Then on a Sunday morning you play football for a league, and that is the Geordie working man's weekend.*

71

This particular male social construction, while fixed within an imaginary sense of the past is expressed in a contemporary form and is challenged by rising participation rates for women on nights out. Friday night is as much a lasses night out in the Bigg Market now and many local women are adamant that their evenings are just as important as well as lively as the mens (see the following case study on women). In these new circumstances versions of an industrial past are linked to a post-industrial present, a process which merges the areas patriarchal economic heritage with the more androgenous experience of modernity. In this kaleidoscope of cultural forms, one can see contradictory representations of exaggerated 'traditional' modes of behaviour alongside the adoption of more contemporary consumption patterns and cosmopolitan attitudes gleaned from the global media (Morrison, 1994).

For example, while patterns of drinking in the Bigg Market have changed due to economic transformations in the drink and leisure industry and the spacial organisation of bars in the city centre, the forms engaged in also have much to do with the reconfirmation of a Geordie identity and involve continuity rather than a complete change with the past. Weekend gang drinking is representative of a kind of working class solidarity and relief from the working week, despite the fact that a significant percentage of locals are neither in full time work or go out with workmates. The adoption of circuit drinking, although a relatively new phenomenon, now involving women, is a perfect symbolic representation of the hard working and hard drinking Geordie.

Our survey did reveal that the one stereotype about Bigg Market regulars that was true was the greater amounts of drink consumed and this was the case for both women and men. However, it is important to note that many of these regulars were older experienced drinkers who in fact know how to hold their alcohol. Contrary to popular opinion the Bigg Market is in fact not full of underage punters, but increasingly caters for the middle of the twenty-something market. This older post adolescent group's engagement in heavy drinking and the ritualization of rites of passage behaviour, is heavily underlined by a desire to project a local identity.

Other contradictions abound here. For example, Harry Enfield's 'bugger all money' character, complete with white tee shirt and cigarettes rolled up in the sleeve, contrasts markedly with the lad with a £125 belt or the young women with an expensive dress. While there may be a kind of hardness expressed here, short sleeves and miniskirts in the dead of winter, dress codes have clearly changed in terms of their quality and price tag. Interestingly enough, the highly charged sexual atmosphere and imagery of the Bigg Market did not in fact live up to its stated reputation, with regulars having a lower number of sexual partners met specifically on a night out than students and other Geordies. Sexism, while clearly existing here, is being increasingly challenged and young women are beginning to demand their own space on nights out. Seemingly boisterous and sometimes aggressive behaviour similarly often masks a lack of pretence, an openness and friendliness amongst and between groups. Finally, while Bigg Market regulars were marginally more likely to be personally involved in a greater number of violent incidents, they were in fact less likely to have witnessed violence on nights out.

A deeper analysis of some of these rituals and contradictions warns against the adoption of unhelpful stereotypes. These negative images often misdirect attention and concern, and also mask the fundamental importance of the Bigg Market as a site of local identity formation. Regulars here were more likely than any group to stress the socialising aspects of going out, including cementing existing friendships, making new friends or just going out to have a laugh. Furthermore, some were even more explicit about how the Bigg Market as a night out was central to their local identity as a Geordie. One local male expressed this point well when asked to recall his best night out ever:

Kevin(L26)   *The night Newcastle were promoted to the first division, it was a Saturday night, we all went out. It was like euphoria everywhere, best atmosphere I have ever been in, it was just amazing. There was nobody in the bars, everybody was just in the Bigg Market itself, out singing, just so happy. That was probably the best night.*

This case study was entitled the Bigg Market and 'beyond', not because the area and the people who inhabit it are unimportant to the analysis. On the contrary, it remains at the heart of the question about how working class cultures survive the end of industrial production and the onslaught of global images and icons to create something alive and unique. In short the Bigg Market has provided and continues to offer the possibility of post-adolescent identities in a somewhat futureless post-industrial locality.

However, it is also clear that the culture of the area is under pressure from various quarters. One obvious influence is increased competition for its more senior clientele in the form of more specialised up-market places increasingly located in the Quayside and Haymarket and the more studentish and casual Station area of the city. Second, is the impact economic and cultural change will continue to have on an already differentiated youth culture. Sections of the local population are beginning to experiment and moved away somewhat from the style and pattern of Bigg Market culture, while some choose to reject it altogether in favour of engagement in more specific music or dance based sub-cultures. If the Bigg Market as a phenomenon is to survive, it will need to recognise and respond to these changes as well as maintain some of its more colourful contradictions. The continuation of a modern Geordie identity may depend, in some sense, on its success to do so.

Student cultures and the city

The inclusion of student cultures and the city in this study is important for a number of reasons. First, they provide a useful contrast and comparison with the local cohort. Second, students make up a significant proportion of users with regard to the night-time economy. Using a University of Newcastle document as a guide, it is estimated that the 22,000 plus students attending the two universities spend an estimated £94 million pounds in the city, of which approximately £14 million goes on entertainment alone. Third, in addition to their financial contribution, students also make a significant impact on the local dance/ music scene and on the maintenance of youth cultures generally.

Throughout the book we have tended to group both university populations together as a student cohort in terms of distinguishing when their responses differ significantly from the local population. While there are sound reasons for dealing with students as an analytical grouping in terms of their predominately middle class social backgrounds and local reaction to the 'university community', we also recognise that differences exist not only between the two educational institutions, but also between student sub-groups within each of the universities. In this short case study, we continue to refer to general student patterns of going out, while also exploring some of the main institutional as well as sub-cultural differences within the population.

Strangely enough considering access to them, there has been very little academic work on student cultures generally (Aggleton, 1987), and we can only begin to scratch the surface of this important area of youth studies. Our cohort consisted of a representative sample of full-time, non-local students from a variety of faculties ranging across years one to four, including two PhD, one M.A and one student nurse. The average age was 21 years, with the majority coming from professional middle-class backgrounds from a variety of localities. While there was little difference between the two university samples in terms of socio-economic status, it is generally recognised that Northumbria recruits a higher percentage of its student body from the north, while Newcastle has a southern bias and a higher percentage of students who have attended public school or received their education through independent schools. A recent article in the high society magazine 'Tatler' (6.6.94) suggested that Newcastle University is increasingly becoming the first choice for many public school students, and according to university statistics for the end of 1991 this sub-group stood at around 26% of the total intake.

Despite these differences, students as a whole have a common position and status in relation to going out in a number of ways. Excluding mature entrants or those living at home, they are independent young adults, free from parental constraints, in charge of their own finances, and able to take advantage of relatively large amounts of 'leisure' time. Student life is also an officially sanctioned post-adolescent transition. In many cases peer group interaction and the development of a satisfactory social life is equal to, if not more important, than academic study. For many, identities in relation to going out is highly significant, and engagement in a variety of forms of student socialising and youth cultures is prevalent.

It is not surprising then to discover that the significance of going out for students actually surpasses that of the general youth population. They go out more frequently than locals, spend a higher percentage of their total income on nights out, and were more likely to say they would feel 'very bad' if they were restricted from going out. What follows is one graphic illustration of the importance of nights out:

RT   *If you were unable to have a night out for say three months how would you feel about it?*

75

Joyce (S21)   *Quite suicidal. Because I'm not the kind of person to sit in at home, I never have been, I don't think I will be.*

These attitudes and behavioural patterns occur despite a wider social context involving cuts in student grants, increased debts and the fact that students were more likely to say that the money they had available actually restricted them from going out as much as they wanted to. Borrowing from friends, understanding parents, and reliance on student loans and bank overdrafts, were the main ways students maintained their commitment to an active social life.

A general student culture can be said to exist not only in relation to their specific social position and attitudes towards nights out, but on two other fronts. First, we have already mentioned their relatively high levels of involvement in club-based dance/ music cultures. Students provide a welcome boost to both the mid-week and weekend club scene and attendance at live music venues in the city. For example, students ranked music and dance as the third most significant reason why they went out and were three times more likely to say this than their local counterparts. A number were heavily into the local club scene, not only as participants but also as DJs and promoters. Students were also one and a half time more likely to prefer live music venues. Despite this support, they were also highly vocal in demanding alternative and more varied clubs specialising in different musical styles as well as calling for more affordable live performance venues.

The second way in which a general student culture persists is in relation to the union bars and the various venues put on at the two universities. In the first year at least, students tend to utilise the union more while trying out other city centre pubs and clubs, with a general pattern of gradually moving away from university bars in particular. This experimentation continues throughout the course of their undergraduate career, with many third year students saying that they now went to quite different places than they did in either first or second year. However, many continued to take advantage of regular club nights at the universities (Northumbria was particularly popular here) and specialist events organised by the student unions involving live music or DJs.

One particular event looked as a case study in this research was a student organised dance night (which shall remain nameless) involving a group of DJ's who play on specific nights at North London

University's Rocket Club as well as appearing bi-monthly at a club in Manchester. While hesitant to label the event a 'rave', many of the main elements were present- a first class light and slide show, an emphasis on dancing and rave music, a 'chill out' area and clear evidence of drug use. While the majority of people there appeared to be very conversant with rave culture, personal observation and conversations with various students subsequently revealed that the event also attracted a wide array of subcultural groups suggesting that certain types of venues attract a more general student as well as local audience (this night was also open to the public). Besides attracting a mix of students and to a lesser extent locals, there is another important point to be made here. Because venues are held on university property and students are not generally seen as a problem by the authorities,[17] there appears to be more scope here for innovation and experimentation in terms of nights out.

While union bars and university venues do provide a setting for the development of a general student identity, institutional differences in terms of ethos, facilities and recruitment practices may mean that Northumbria and Newcastle entrants have slightly different experiences as students in the city. Due to the fact that Northumbria recruits more widely from the North East, means that students there from outside the area are likely to have more contact with locals students than their Newcastle counterparts. Because of a south bias in recruitment, Newcastle students were less likely to be exposed to locals and on the basis of accent alone, sometimes were more likely to stick out in a mixed venue. Without referring directly to the 'other' university, one Northumbria student intimated about the 'type' of student who was less likely to fit in with locals:

Sam (S21)   *I think there is a certain type of student who will definitely just make no effort at all with the er, locals. I'll give you an example, there's a couple that's just moved into Sidney Grove, which is where I live in Fenham and they're quite a well to do middle class couple. But they said they'd moved out of Jesmond because the er, students that are there are just so arrogant and there is no sense of community or anything. And they're just really snobbish about the whole thing and I think its that type of student.*

77

Club nights at Northumbria were popular amongst certain Newcastle students and a number suggested that they actually preferred the former to their own union because of the different atmosphere. While somewhat of a generalisation, it appeared from what many respondent were saying that demarcations between students were less significant at Northumbria, while Newcastle was characterised by a more hierarchical or at least divided student population.

This brings us to the final point of this case study and that is the recognition that both university populations are internally divided into recognisable subgroups. While the local population often tends to view university entrants as a unified group, students themselves are keenly aware of particular sub-cultural groupings. Two examples of identifiable student sub-groups were 'agric's (agriculture students) and sloanes (or 'yahs'):

Rob (S23)   *From what I hear sort of just drinking ridiculous amounts and peer pressure and being forced to drink pints of beer. Persons throwing up all over the place, wrecking and pulling things to pieces. I think its very much tradition and the reputation, everyone immediately knows about the drinking habits of Newcastle agrics, the reputation goes before you. They're sort of a mix of sloanes and young farmers and you get a group of them like that and, its the rugby as well.*

Mick (S21)   *Oh gosh, just home counties, upper middle class, daddy's an accountant, BMW sort of thing. Sort of nice jumpers and caps at silly angles and hockey sticks and stuff, stupid shoes and things like that. And never have a bag, always folders and papers and books in their hand, or under their arm, they don't carry a bag. They've all got cars.*

Other groups, in addition to agrics and sloanes, that students themselves identified in interviews, through either symbols (i.e. clothing, style, music) or attitudes or beliefs, were ravers, crusties (or new agers), hardcore, LGB (lesbian, gay and bisexual society), metallers, sporties, and a general category of 'ordinary' student.

In the course of conducting this research we were unable to explore these divisions in any detail and hence can only provide some general ideas for further study. First, we have already mentioned that some of this differentiation is actually institutional in character and university societies may act to reinforce student hierarchies. Second, it is clear that at least some of this differentiation is class based, with sub-groups like sloanes and sporties more likely to come from public or independent school backgrounds, while 'ordinary' students are generally products of the comprehensive system. Finally, student cultures are increasingly becoming fragmented by the same processes of economic and cultural change experienced by our local cohort.

Uncertainty in the graduate labour market, combined with a heightened availability of consumption symbols, provides a context for the development of a range of alternative identities around sexual orientation, unemployment, politics, leisure, not to mention a plethora of music, dance and drug based lifestyles. Clearly, all of these factors require further investigation as do the wide range of student sub-cultures mentioned only briefly here.

Alternative spaces and lifestyles

One of the strong themes which emerged in terms of going out was not only the idea of differentiation amongst youth style and culture but the notion of 'alternative' places. Our respondents talked about the 'hippy run', 'hardcore' gigs, 'biker' pubs, 'resurrections', 'indie' club nights and the 'Pink Triangle' to mention but a few. Clearly, it was impossible to even begin to study a handful of these in any detail. Here we specifically focus in on two examples of spaces outside of the 'mainstream'- a 'new age' pub and gay and lesbian culture and nightlife.

Hippies and a 'new age' pub

The connection between an alternative style and place is perhaps best examined by looking at a specific establishment and its use by a particular youth cultural grouping. The Doll House (name changed) is a well known city centre pub with live music and, according to one of the guide books on Newcastle, has an 'idiosyncratic' clientele of 'old rockers, goths, and hippies'. Our fieldwork revealed the existence of all of these groups, but it revolves specifically around the latter group described as hippies, 'crusties' or those loosely influenced by the 'new-age' phenomenon.[18] The pubs casual decor, which some would describe as 'seedy', and its patron's association with a certain type of post-punk musical style and liberal attitude towards soft drug use, sets it apart from some of its contemporaries as a bona-fide alternative nightspot.

The question of whether or not this fraction of the Doll House's clientele is a subculture depends largely on one's definition and theoretical perspective. One of the difficulties with previous subcultural paradigms were their over-reliance on highly visible and tightly focused class-based examples like skinheads, teddy boys and punks. Furthermore subcultures increasingly became seen purely as styles to be identified and 'decoded' (Hebdige, 1979), rather than looking at young adults' own meanings and identifications. In this case study we would argue that stylistic modes of communication, engagement in certain focal activities, and common belief systems are operating here and are expressed and reinforced within a particular setting or 'locale'.

While there is not the space here to outline all of the elements of this cultural identification in detail, they should at least be mentioned. Common sets of values exist in relation to a rejection of traditional political parties, particularly the Conservatives and a general commitment towards anti-sexist, anti-racist, anti-homophobic and pro-animal rights ideas. A number of the young people we interviewed were involved in the Poll Tax movement and similar number were currently active in various ecology groups and organisations opposing the Criminal Justice Bill. The group also rejected traditional views concerning the work ethic with employment often being seen as a means to an end, while unemployment was viewed creatively as leisure time, particularly with respect to travelling to music events and festivals. In terms of gender relations and make-up of the group, young women were found in equal numbers to men and there was an implicit philosophy of equality between the sexes.

Stylistically, the subculture was identifiable in terms of its adoption of second hand clothes, tattoos, multiple ear and sometimes nose piercings and some form of dreadlocks or 'punkish' hair style. While many experiment with a range of drugs (speed, LSD, magic mushrooms), the staple substance used is cannabis, which was often smoked openly in the pub. A number were involved in the local music scene and the pub reflected this interest by providing live music, which while usually loud and 'punky', also incorporated reggae, folk and ethnic influences.

The idea of a subculture involves not just common experiences and stylistic symbols, but also contains unwritten rules of social interaction within the group and identification of the culture externally by 'outsiders'. Both of these features were present with respect to the subgroup in question. With regard to the first point, the 'invasion' of the Doll House by a local group of lads allegedly involved in the 'hard' end of the West city drug market, resulted in the creation of a 'bad atmosphere' according to the regular clientele, due to their transgression and failure to recognise the cultural ambience of the pub. Women members of the subculture were particularly affected and experienced verbal and physical harassment during this period, a situation which was largely foreign to them.

Second, it was clear that a 'group sense' was recognised both internally by members themselves as well as externally by people outside of the culture. In fact, one of the regulars sought to describe the subculture in terms of other people's perceptions, while outsiders were able to identify the group at least stylistically:

Mandy (L27)   *I suppose other people would describe them [us] as alternative. They're [us] probably more politically aware. I suppose people view them [us] as hippies.*

Jan (L29)   *The Doll's House is a bit em, its very new age, there's a lot of bikers that get there as well, but there's an awful lot of crusties, you know, like err, a crustie is a white person with dreadlocks. A crustie is a new age traveller with dreads and a dog on a string type of thing you know.*

While there were a few other places where this subculture frequented, known locally as the 'hippy run', the group in question tended to see the Doll House as their main space, and most criticised a lack of alternative places in the city. Their main pattern of going out was to simply drift into the pub to drink, smoke cannabis and perhaps watch a band. In a sense, their subcultural identity was reflected and reinforced by their marginalisation not only to a particular area of the city, but to a specific establishment. This general idea of marginality is also central to the next case study concerning gay and lesbian night-time culture in the city.

We have previously mentioned gay and lesbian culture and nightlife under the heading of the 'divided city'. This short case study delves more deeply into the topic primarily in terms of the notion of identity and access to space. Additionally, this is an ideal place to voice some of the issues and concerns expressed by that proportion of the sample who identified themselves as gay, lesbian or bisexual, in terms of their own experiences of night-time facilities offered in the city. The analysis is aided by a recent book documenting gay men's experiences of urban life (Whittle, 1994), which incidently contains an article on the city of Newcastle (Lewis, 1994).

The centrality of nightlife as a part of gay lifestyle and identity is unmistakable. As Hindle (1994, p. 11) argues, pubs clubs and discos 'are probably the most important single feature of a gay community'. This is particularly the case in those cities which do not have a visible territory and infrastructure where gay and lesbians live, work, shop and socialise. The most well known and studied example of a gay community is the Castro area of San Deafened in San Francisco (Castells, 1983), with developments in other cities like the gay gentrification of the 'Cabbagetown' area of Toronto gaining attention. The emergence of a visible gay community in Britain began in the 1970s, and while London initially attracted a higher percentage of homosexuals than elsewhere in the country and provided some of the first gay venues, businesses and support groups, Manchester's 'Gay Village' is often held up as the U.K. prototype in terms of providing a recognisable community in a delimited physical space.

The gay and lesbian community in Newcastle, on the other hand, could be said to be marginalised on a number of levels. As Lewis (1994) states in his article entitled 'A Sociological Pub Crawl Around Gay Newcastle', the city itself is separated economically, culturally and politically from the rest of the country. The net effect of this separation, fuelled by the region's masculine economic and cultural history, explains the areas rigid gender stereotyping and the persistence of anti-gay and homophobic feelings. As such, gay space itself becomes segregated or limited to particular places, for example commercial venues like gay pubs or clubs. These places themselves are often marginalised by being in less popular and often run-down areas of the city ('the margins').

While the formation of this space creates an atmosphere of safety and security for the expression of an alternative lifestyle, gay and lesbians are effectively excluded from being 'themselves' elsewhere. One of our gay respondents discussed this feeling when walking through certain parts of the city centre:

Stan (L31)   *Walking back from er, when I used to go alone, I used to walk back and I used to get nervous at the lads that were drunk. The Bigg Market and places like that.*

While none of the gay and lesbians we spoke to admitted to being attacked because of their sexual orientation, they did complain that not only were they unable to be openly gay in straight bars in Newcastle, but that their own nightlife facilities were in marginal and somewhat dangerous areas of the city.

Although not immune to prejudice and homophobic attacks, Newcastle University's Lesbian, Gay and Bisexual Society (LGB) and Northumbria's Students Union Globe are two examples of support and pressure groups which provide some sense of community and solidarity amongst gay, lesbian, and bisexual students. With respect to the former university, various events such as Pink Triangle Week (a raising awareness exercise) and a Valentine's disco for the LGB are two examples of providing activities and raising gay issues. Both university societies provide an important clientele for gay venues in the city, and although it was generally felt that Newcastle had a recognisable and lively gay scene, it was far from perfect:

Emily (L28)   *It [the Pink Triangle] needs to be extended, it needs to take up more space. I would like to see it in a nicer area, you know, rather than flung out at the end of the city.*

The inclusion of bisexuals into both student organisations, and the discussion of students generally, raises important questions over the issue of mixed venues versus the notion of separate spheres. The gay scene in Newcastle is located primarily in the station area of the city, in a geographically compact area known by some as the 'Pink Triangle'. At last count, there were two gay clubs, and five gay pubs, with a couple of additional places putting on special lesbian or gay nights. While certain pubs and clubs are well recognised as gay places by the majority of the heterosexual population, and sometimes avoided, it is mixed venues that raises questions about bi-sexuality and the 'straight' invasion of gay space.

Anecdotal evidence suggests that some women prefer the sanctity of gay bars, where they can be free from verbal and physical harassment, and the term 'fag-hag' has been used to describe heterosexual women who prefer to hang out with gay men. Additionally, a recent journalistic article on Manchester's Gay Village, states that various subcultural groups, including some types of students, choose to frequent gay venues because of the casual atmosphere and general lack of violence and disorder (The Observer 29.8.93).

Some of the gay and lesbian people we interviewed welcomed mixed venues and suggested that there should be more, while actually complaining about strict 'gays only' admissions policies. While bisexuals are included in the two university societies and are seemingly an important connection between the gay and the straight world, David Bell (1994) has recently argued that bi-sexuality is a double marginalisation in terms of both space and identity. In other words, they are often shunned by the dominant heterosexual world and viewed with extreme suspicion by sections of the gay community. One young bi-sexual student was quick to point out how sexual segregation in terms of nights out left him to choose between lifestyles, neither of which completely appealed to him:

Julian (S22)   *I think Newcastle definitely needs more of a gay village, and I think its a really good thing because that's when people first 'come out'. But I think you have to be careful though, because a lot of people would come out as gay, and this has happened to a couple of my friends, and they come out as gay and that's all their life. They only know gay people, they only go to gay clubs and I think that's really sad, because I have an absolute whale of a time with my straight friends and that's not just because I'm bisexual, because loads of my gay friends do as well. You can't just have a little village over here which is only for gay people. I think the best sort of place to go would be somewhere where it didn't really matter, you could be who you wanted to be.*

Bi-sexuality then complicates the issue of identity and territory and inadvertently raises questions about the politics of space. As argued earlier in the section on the 'divided city', there are really two contrary arguments for having a gay village. One positive approach which suggests that separate space is necessary for the development of gay identity and to ensure support and solidarity, and a more negative versions based on a kind of sexual apartheid. It is apparent from our research that while the Pink Triangle very much provides the former, many gays, lesbians and bisexuals are seeking to break free from the boundaries of the latter perspective.

Ladies only: young women and the city

Throughout this book we have sought to highlight the role gender plays in structuring women and men's nights out. In this short case study we want to focus specifically on young local women's experiences to highlight the huge social significance changing gender relations are having on the future of city life. The persistence and indeed strengthening of 'ladies only' nights out has been recognised in the popular media, but has received little sustained analysis.

Despite the existence of both historical legacies and contemporary barriers, young adult working class women have made great leaps forward in terms of reforming their identity in relation to going out in the city. Numerous commentators have noted that in many towns and cities in England, Scotland and Ireland, women are found in equal numbers to men and exude a powerful influence on the night time economy and culture. In this study local women surpassed their male counterparts in terms of the frequency with which they visit the city, as well as spend a higher percentage of their income on nights out. They were also twice as likely as local men to say they would feel 'very bad' if restricted from going out, and two-thirds said they would go out either the same or more often if they were married.

Some of these findings are indeed surprising considering the formidable obstacles young working class women still face economically, domestically and culturally. As we have argued, while the changing regional labour market has provided some local women with a sense of self-esteem and confidence, it by no means has offered them any kind of financial security. Domestically, young women are reliant on parents, partners or shared households and their leisure time is more likely to be interrupted by their higher involvement

85

in doing household chores. And finally, continuing assumptions about female sexuality means that many young women have to put up with verbal and sometimes physical harassment on nights out.

The identity transformation young women have made in the movement away from their confinement to the domestic community to consumption in the city is both powerful and fragile, and contains future possibilities as well as constraining historical legacies. For example, female patterns of going out continue to be structured around the home, for example the ritual of getting ready, and in some cases are influenced by domestic expectations of either 'finding a man' or celebrating the future confines of domestic bliss (the so called 'hen night').

Some were also forced to relay financially on their boyfriend or husband for nights out, while many young women accompanied by a female best friend were assumed to be 'available' and only out on a night for men's pleasure. While these older domestic and sexual ideologies persist, they are overshadowed by some substantial shifts in women's perceptions of a good night out and an increased growth of female solidarity.

The importance of women socialising in the contemporary context of the city is expressed by two main research finding. First, local women are those most likely to go out in single-sex groups and second, 'socialising with friends' was their single most important reason for having nights out. The significance attributed to both of these points is expressed best by some of our female interviewees themselves:

RT   *If you had to focus in on one thing that going out means to you personally, what would it be?*

Meryl(L19) *Going out with me friends, enjoying meself, might be going out for a meal and having a gossip (...) Cos I've got a big circle of friends. Sometimes all the girls will go out, like tonight its a girl's birthday, so there'll be ten girls going out. On Thursday I always go out with girlfriends.*

RT   *When you go out on girls nights out, do you ever meet up with blokes, or do you really stick together?*

Meryl   *Stick together.*

86

Jan (L29)   *It's a shame really cos we used to have such*
                     good nights out when we used to all go out in a
                     foursome with w' two other girlfriends. That was
                     great, such good fun. Because we just laughed all
                     the time, we weren't interested in men, because
                     like I was married, me friend was married, me
                     other friend was married, and the last one, she
                     was quite a plain girl who was quite fat, and she
                     wasn't, she used to pretend not to be interested
                     in men, because she couldn't get them basically,
                     you know. So we went out, we weren't interested
                     in men, we weren't relying on men for w'
                     conversation.

Increasingly, young women's movement into this public sphere has
been matched by a growing demand to socialise in exclusively female
circles and to insist on their own space independent of men. Examples
of ladies only nights, actively designed to exclude men, were clearly
evident during participant observation visits to the city centre. One
strategy adopted was to move away from going out just with a
girlfriend to a large group or gang of women, mirroring the pattern
adopted by many local men. Some respondents also mentioned that
they would chose to frequent pubs which were women friendly or go
to gay pubs and bars to avoid male harassers. The idea of going out
as an extended socialising ritual, has become an increasingly
important forum for what young women have been doing for years
within the more invisible confines of the home and community. The
literal process of 'coming out' and revealing a collective female public
identity, is the product of a number of processes.

First, there have been changes in the assertion and expression of
female sexuality. While sexual freedom has been personified and
indeed 'demonised' in the characters of the 'fat slags' in the local
comic **The Viz**, the real issue here is that many men are threatened
by the fact that young women are apparently more in control of their
sexual feelings and identity. Rather than being promiscuous, local
women are in fact 'choosier' about potential sexual partners, yet more
relaxed with their sexuality. The small number who mentioned that one
of the reasons they went out was to meet a member of the opposite
sex, expressed this view comfortably, not ashamedly.

Second, there has been a weakening of traditional expectations
concerning meeting a partner and marriage amongst young working

class women. In other words the older pattern of 'deffing out', dumping your girl friend when you meet the right bloke (Griffin, 1985), has broken down somewhat. Many demanded that female friendships and going out with other women continue during courtship. Part of the reason for this may be due to a lack of 'eligible' young men in economically deprived areas, but is also connected in some sense to young women's changing economic position and views about their future as wives and mothers. Some local women were becoming much more selective about their options in this regard. One 'thirty-something' woman we spoke to put it this way:

Meg (L31)   *I have a reasonable job, a house and mortgage and a car, so I don't really need a bloke around. If I meet someone its on my own terms.*

Now while not all young women were in this position, it is clear that some have begun to step outside of established female roles and social expectations concerning marriage.

   The mixture of freedom and solidarity and continuing barriers and traditions, means that the ways in which young local working class women express themselves publicly on nights out is somewhat contradictory. On the one hand, there is often a strong female 'group sense' and an attempt to separate themselves off from men. One young woman mentions how some young men find this idea hard to deal with:

Lynn (L29)   *One young lad who tried to dance with me, they just like muscle in, they don't sort of do anything. They just muscle in and try to dance and he spoilt it a bit because he tried to get me off on me own to dance and I didn't want to. I just wanted to dance with my friends [a group of women].*

This separation may be expressed by sticking loyally to the group, displaying an obvious preference to women's company, and parodying female qualities of closeness and support. On the other hand, the forms they adopt are also influenced by class and as such, some of their activities and behaviours appear to mirror those of the lads on a night out. In other words, 'equal opportunity' in class terms is about being able to do exactly what the men do. Ironically ladies only nights can take on many of the characteristics of the traditional lads night out with heavy drinking, boisterous and sometimes aggressive behaviour, and fairly obvious expressions of sexuality. On the negative side, it is interesting to note that local women are more likely than men to have been involved in a fight on a night out.

Despite some of these contradictions, going out as a source of identity has clearly increased for many young working class women, and has given them a heightened public presence. While older patterns persist, new possibilities and cultural forms are emerging. This is not to argue that Geordie women are somehow totally liberated, nor should anyone be complacent about the continuing obstacles young women face economically, sexually and culturally. Dangers within the night time economy persist for young women and include examples of verbal and physical harassment, and reports of abuse by male doormen.

Economically, local women have a long way to go in order to ensure an independent future and although there are wider changes in the domestic economy and household, there are still strong expectations here. Those women we spoke to who were married and had children, reminded us that there is a slight contradiction between rhetoric and reality when it comes to mixing home and social life. While it is important to celebrate some of the unleashed potential generated by ladies only nights out, it is equally central to recognise that traditional transitions are being delayed not abolished, and many barriers remain.

'About 20 million British people will return this year from a European break in resorts or cities where it is commonplace to munch a sandwich and sip a beer or coffee at 2 am...Conversely, many of Britain's foreign visitors will find the only late night choice to be hostile city streets, curry houses catering mainly for inebriated young men and pubs or clubs turning everybody out at the same time'

Jon Trickett, Labour Leader, Leeds City Council (Guardian 17.9.93)

6. Policy Suggestions

Overall, what came across during the course of this research was that Newcastle generally was regarded positively as a city with a vibrant nightlife. Young local adults in particular often expressed a great pride in their 'toon', as it is affectionately known, and their assessment of Newcastle as a place to go out largely reproduced this favourable attitude. Students, in a slightly different way, also tended to view the city in a positive light. This is not to say that the city is free from problems or impervious to improvements by any means, but it should provide a wider context for 'constructive' criticism and policy suggestions which follow. We begin this section by analysing our sample's views on what they felt were the best and worst aspects of going out in Newcastle, as well as comparing nightlife here with other major English and Scottish cities.

Comparing Newcastle nightlife

The best aspect of Newcastle nightlife comes under the general heading of 'atmosphere'. Around 40% of the sample suggested that this was the best aspect about going out in the city. The most appropriate way to express this feeling is to quote from some local young adults:

Dee (L21)   *Everybody in the North East is very patriotic, I think to their area. My sister's boyfriend came up the end of last week and he was saying you know, how everybody seems to be sort of together. You get a lot of good people you know and you can just stand and have a really good chat with them and a good time and everybody tries to be happy.*

Gaz (L22)　　*You go out for a good night in Newcastle, you're out with a couple of friends, and everyone wants to have a good time as well. I mean they join in with you or you join in with them.*

Included within the general category of atmosphere was the idea that the people of Newcastle were friendly, unpretentious and most importantly, knew how to have a good time. Geordies were as likely, if not more so than students, to say these things about themselves.

The other prominent positive feature mentioned by the sample was the physical environment of the city, expressed primarily in relation to the proximity of bars, pubs and clubs in the centre. Interesting enough this particular feature was also used to explain both the atmosphere generated and the patterns of behaviour adopted on nights out. In other words, young adults themselves are keenly aware of how the spacial layout and organisation of the city centre provides a context for certain types of behaviour, feelings and social interaction. While largely in agreement on these issues, students were as likely to assess Newcastle positively in terms of the variety of nightlife it offered, as they were to mention its highly charged and friendly atmosphere.

Regarding the worst aspect of going out in Newcastle, a number of general themes emerged. Fifteen percent cited a lack of alternative night-time provision as the worst thing about the city, while the same percentage mentioned violence as a problem. A further 10% said expense was an issue and 8% mentioned overcrowding and long queues. Interestingly enough, 13% of Geordies themselves said that local people's attitudes were the worst aspect of Newcastle nightlife, citing things like 'excessively macho' and 'small mindedness'. The same percentage of students suggested that segregation between themselves and locals was the worst thing about going out in the city.

When asked if they felt Newcastle was lacking anything in terms of nightlife nearly half of the sample answered in the affirmative. The main response focused in on a lack of good clubs. With one or two exceptions, it was felt that Newcastle's club scene was very predictable and didn't cater for the variety of musical tastes and dance cultures that existed:

Ellen (S21)   *In the last six months its really picked up a lot and but the people that own the clubs tend to be, em, they really just want the money and they're not really interested in giving people quality nights out, which is the thing I think is really lacking.*

In conjunction with this, the city was seen as lacking a big live music venue and a lack of alternative places such as cafes, pubs with live music, and places catering for particular sub-cultural styles (see the sub-section on alternative provision for details). Overall, the split between those who were generally satisfied with the state of Newcastle's nightlife and those who wanted something different, was as evident amongst the local population as it was within the student community.

Many of the positive and negative feature of Newcastle nightlife were reiterated when we asked our sample to compare the city with other English/ Scottish cities. Again, locals generally rated Newcastle very highly in terms of atmosphere when comparing it with going out in other cities. As one local women lyrically said, *'its simply the best'*. The positiveness of student comparisons depended very much upon whether they were from quiet rural areas and smaller provincial towns or from larger more cosmopolitan cities. Pub-wise Newcastle rated very highly with its variety and proximity of places being its most distinguishing features. It was again with respect to clubs and alternative venues that the city appeared to flag in comparison to other locations. Manchester, Nottingham, Leeds and Glasgow for example were more highly rated in terms of clubbing with respect to both variety and atmosphere. Part of the issue concerned the different licensing hours adopted in particular cities, but also related to the diversity of musical/ dance and fashion tastes being catered for.

Service satisfaction

In the course of this research we sought to quantify young adult's views about the quality of service they receive on nights out. We asked our respondents to provide a score ranging from very good, good, average, below average and poor, to indicate the level of service they experienced from various personnel involved in the night time economy. Included within this group were bar managers, bar staff, doormen, metro staff, bus and taxi drivers and the police. In presenting this information, we found it most useful to group responses according to whether punters found the service either above or below average, although at times it is useful to highlight the percentage of scores in specific categories (for comments see **Transcribed Interviews 4**).

With the exception of Metro staff, pub and club managers were the group least likely to receive any response from our sample. Many stated that they had no contact or dealings with the management or that managers were not really visible on nights out. While this might be seen as a positive endorsement of the effective running of bars and clubs, a number of people commented that they would like to see managers circulate more amongst the clientele. This invisibility may indeed have something to do with the lack of 'untied' public houses in the city where landlords might be more apt to cultivate a loyal custom. The fact that a high proportion of bars and pubs in the city centre are owned by a small number of large companies who have a captive market, may mean that management is largely a financial rather than a social activity.

Despite this, 38% of those who responded gave bar managers a better than average score, while 46% said they were at least average. Of these, the majority cited efficient organisation of the pub or club and a lack of trouble as the main reasons why they felt management was effective. Only 16% felt that the treatment or service they received from managers was below average. The main complaints here had to do with what customers felt were arbitrary rules and regulations like unexplained dress restrictions and no dancing policies amongst others. Overall, while most customers felt unable to rate a managers performance, a significant majority of those who could felt that managers were doing a good job.

Everyone, on the other hand, had contact with bar staff and felt able to rate them in terms of level of service. Bar staff in city centre pubs and clubs received one of the highest ratings with 60% of our sample saying they provided above average service, with a further 38% stating that they rated them average. The main comments as to why the service was above average centred on efficiency, friendliness and fairness. Many punters were also aware of the fact that tending bar was hard work and not particularly well paid. Only 2% felt that Newcastle bar staff was below average, with the main comments

TRANSCRIBED INTERVIEWS 4

NIGHTLIFE SERVICE SATISFACTION

Managers:

Ken (L30)
: *They tend to be a bit indifferent to the customers because at times there are floods of people waiting. I know people who have been owners as well as managers and of course they seem to be far more, they're the people who are the best host and hostesses.*

Kevin (L25)
: *They make me sick that they don't let people in with training shoes on. Like you know 'dappers', you know like deck shoes type of affair. You could pay £60 for a pair and they wont let you in.*

Bar Staff:

Sue (L19)
: *Sometimes they're ratty, I mean its just cos they're busy though.*

Doug (L31)
: *Well bar staff, its all very impersonal, there are so many people out. Obviously in the city centre they are just purely there to get through as many customers as possible, so you don't really expect good service.*

Doormen:

Lynn (L29)
: *They're such macho pigs, I hate them.*

Paul (L16)
: *They let young people in. Cos I'm young meself, aa don't really say much.*

Gaz (L22)
: *I think they're entry-exit technicians. With the pubs you tend to see them mingle, but if you go to any places like the clubs a lot of them are above their station.*

Metro/ Bus and Taxi Drivers:

Carl (L18)
: *Metro inspectors, they are right bastards. they kind of want to be policeman but aren't clever enough. Metro staff are ok.*

Dee (L21)
: *Bus drivers? They're good, they're always happy and friendly and stuff and let you on with your chips.*

Carol (S19)
: *I've been in taxis a few times and sometimes they're really friendly, chat to you about what they've been doing.*

ranging from unfairness to a lack of interest in customer needs. As expected, doormen, or bouncers, generated strong reactions from the sample. While just over half the sample rated them as doing at least an average job, only 30% gave them an above average score. Forty-nine percent felt that they were performing below average and within this category 23% actually gave them a poor score (the highest for all personnel involved on a night out). Amongst local men there appeared to be a grudging respect for doormen, while local women were somewhat less enamoured in their assessment. Students, specifically males, tended to be much more negative arguing that many doormen were anti-student and were most likely to take this feeling out on them. Some students refused to go to bars that had doormen and overall a number of people interviewed recalled 'unnecessary' incidents of violence involving bouncers. While the door-registration scheme has apparently reduced the number of these incidents, it is clear that a lot remains to be done in improving relations between doormen and customers, particularly students.

Transportation is an important part of nights out and we asked our sample to comment on all three of the main forms of travel-Metro, bus and taxis. The Metro appeared to be the least used but was given the highest above average score with 62% rating it in this category (14% also rated it average). Generally, it was seen to be clean, efficient, on time and staff were mostly friendly and helpful. However, views were somewhat polarised with 24% actually giving it a below average score. Comments here focused on the fact that it should run later, there was not adequate security and some staff, particularly those checking tickets, were sometimes 'over-zealous'.

A relatively higher percentage of the sample used buses and taxis, although students, because they were more likely to live centrally, often walked to and from the city. Bus drivers received the best cumulative rating, with 96% saying they provided either an average or above average service. The main comments centred around their sense of humour and tolerance regarding food, boisterous behaviour and sometimes overlooking difficulties making up the exact fare. Only 4% stated that they felt bus drivers provided a below average service. Taxi drivers also received a good overall rating with 87% saying they provided an average or above average service. Again their sense of humour and tolerance were the main sources of a positive evaluation. Thirteen percent rated their performance as below average with the main complaints being over-charging, going the long way around and grumpiness.

Policing the city/ CCTV cameras

The final indicator of service satisfaction was the performance of police. While many respondents did not have any contact with the police and felt unable to comment, overall the view was that they were doing a reasonable job during nights out. Eighty percent of the sample felt that the police were doing either an average or above average job. Generally they were seen as largely unobtrusive, good humoured and tolerant of exuberant behaviour displayed on nights out. The general approach could be characterised as 'community policing'. One story told to us gives new meaning to the term:

Viv (L25)   *My friend always goes to the Bigg Market to drink, and before we went to a night club I would always meet her at the top, because I wouldn't go there. She met this policeman, chatted him up, took him home. Still on duty, took him home, had sex with him, and then he went back on duty and she went to the nightclub.*

On a more serious note, many respondents, including young women, felt it was important that the police were present in they city to deter any problems from arising. On the other hand, it is worth noting that of all seven services rated on a night out, the police received the third lowest above average score and the third highest below average score. One in five of our sample felt that the police were doing a below average job policing the city centre during nights out. One of the main complaints concerned inconsistencies in the availability of police and an over-reaction in situations where problems did not really exist:

Nadim (L24)   *They tend to be a bit heavy-handed at the wrong times. Its like they've got figures to hit, they need to make some arrests, they make some arrests. At other times when there is like a lot of violence and a big fight breaks out somewhere, you tend not to see them till its all been dealt with.*

Decker (L19)   *Some of my friends have had bad run ins and I've been pulled over a few times just because of the way I dress. I'll tell you the worst thing is, a lad called Sam, he's black, me and him were walking*

round and the pair of w' got pulled over and got
the most grief off a policeman I've ever had in my
entire life.

A small section of our sample were clearly anti-police in terms of either previous run ins or due to their wider political orientation. There was also a feeling amongst some students that the police seemed more aggressive when dealing with them as potential suspects and less sensitive to their needs when it came to protection and safety. In addition to a significant police presence, the other major forms of policing nightlife in the city are both technological rather than human. The first example is the Pubwatch Scheme, set up in 1992, which involves the use of electronic pagers to alert both police and other pub owners of potential trouble groups. Managers and police are able to respond quickly to situations and information about the identity of perpetrators can be quickly passed on to other bars to avoid trouble spreading. Preliminary indications are that the scheme has been effective in containing anti-social behaviour and ensuring a quick police reaction. The other main form of technological policing is the Close Circuit Television (CCTV) system. Launched in December 1992 and funded by local business, the Department of the Environment, Newcastle City Council and the Northumbria Police, it consists of 16 cameras spread strategically throughout the city, with a central control room at Market Street police station. Cameras are present in all of the main drinking areas in the city, including the Haymarket, Quayside and Bigg/ Groat Market.

We asked our sample whether they agreed or disagreed with the use of CCTV to police the city centre on nights out and under what circumstances they felt it was effective. Seventy-seven percent agreed that the cameras should be used, 20% disagreed and the remaining 3% didn't know. The main reasons given in support of the CCTV were that it served as a deterrent, it provided valuable evidence in the event of a serious crime being committed, and it resulted in the police being able to respond more quickly to disturbances. Generally, those who supported the use of the cameras stated that they felt safer in the city centre now and they dismissed liberty and freedom arguments on the basis that the cameras were benign if you were acting reasonably. Curiously enough local men were most likely to be in favour of the CCTV system, with 100% answering in the affirmative, while over 90% of student women also agreed with the use of cameras.

Of the one in five who disagreed with the CCTV, the main arguments raised were the issue of civil liberties, the lack of evidence regarding deterrence, and the fact that the camera were being used to control young people rather than deal with serious crime. Many saw the cameras as an example of increased social control and infringement on human rights, a kind of 'Orwellian 1984 effect'. Others called into question the idea that CCTV would actually deter someone who was already drunk or violent from carrying out an attack. Some had friends who had been spotted by the cameras and picked up and charged for relatively minor offenses, like urinating in public. Most of our sample admitted a lack of knowledge about the CCTV system, and many suggested that they required further information and evidence about its use and effectiveness.

Police records themselves and an independent analysis of the CCTV system conducted at Newcastle University, demonstrate the complexities of the debate about use and deterrence. While recorded crime appeared to drop by 33% in the city centre from 1991 to 1993, the reduction primarily consisted of a decrease in crimes of property (burglary and car theft). Alcohol related arrests, including drunk and disorderly and wounding/ assaults remained fairly stable, and even went up slightly over this three year period, although recently a police spokesman suggested that there had been a 20% reduction of assaults in the last year. On the other hand, an independent analysis of the CCTV cameras over a six month period from April to September 1993, showed that only about 18% of incidents logged involved what might be termed offenses against the person, with just 13 cases (only 2% of the total) involving an offensive weapon (Centre for Research on Crime, Policing and the Community, 1993). The largest single category of incidents recorded was labelled 'suspicious youths', with less than 10% of these cases resulting in arrests.

While the cameras clearly can provide valuable evidence of serious crimes against the person, it is also obvious that these constitute a minority of incidents in the city centre. It is also unclear from the figures available to categorically say that the CCTV system alone acts as an effective deterrent against violent crime. Those who argue that the cameras are primarily designed to protect property and monitor 'less serious' crimes and activities in the city centre would also appear to have some evidence for making these assertions. While more detailed research is needed on the CCTV system, policy-makers would be equally advised to pursue a range of strategies designed to tackle the roots of violent and anti-social behaviour generally.

Licensing

One of the most contentious policy areas concerning nightlife in Britain are the present licensing laws. The debate about licensing is a long and tortuous one and has recently come back on to the agenda with respect to two new pieces of legislation. The argument is not simply one about actual 'drinking time', but also hints at wider issues of social control, economic considerations, widening access, and broader cultural changes in leisure and consumption patterns (Lovatt, 1994). Britain has a long history of regulation with regard to the sale and consumption of alcohol, as well as the restriction of licensing hours. For example the Christian temperance movement of the late 19th century and the Defense of the Realm Act during the first world war instituted restrictions on the time available to consume alcohol (The Guardian 7.2.95). Since this time there has been only a gradual liberalisation of the drinking laws, leaving Britain far behind some of its European counterparts in terms of licensing hours. In 1961 laws were relaxed allowing more outlets to sell alcohol, the 1977 Clayson Report heralded the extension of licensing hours in certain premises in Scotland, and by 1988 all day opening and extra time on Sundays was passed.

More recently, changes to legally allow children into pubs has been passed as well as all day Sunday openings. Local magistrates continue to have the power to grant extended licenses to clubs and pubs according to 'local need'. One recent example of this was Manchester's extension of city centre pub opening hours until 12:00 in the month preceding their bid to host the 1996 Olympics.

Young adults in our sample were categorically in favour of extending licensing hours with 77% answering in the affirmative. Students were slightly more likely to say this with 80% arguing for an extensions. The major reason for extending licensing hours given by young adults in our sample concerned the changing style of British nightlife drinking culture. The majority felt that the present system created a 'hurry up and get it down your neck' approach to drinking, while extended hours would create a much more relaxed and restrained night out:

Margi (L29)   *You'd probably go out later I would imagine. Because when we used to go to Glasgow and the nightclubs used to open till 4:00, we were often drinking Pepsi by that time. We weren't*

necessarily drinking alcohol, but we loved the fact
that it was open till that time. So you're not
necessarily drinking more, but its all within your
own limits you know. If the Mayfair was open till
4:00 I wouldn't have that much more to drink,
maybe an extra pint or something.

Other reasons given for extended hours were that it would lead to less drunkenness, violence and anti-social behaviour, relieve pressure on services like taxis, food outlets and buses, and people would have the option of going out later on in the evening for a drink. One important perspective on the extension of licensing was focused on the social control element of the debate:

Cal (S26)   *Because I think that the laws as they are, are a*
form of social control. They control when you can
drink certainly in public spaces and they still fit
within the pattern of its almost an informal
curfew, that it is expected that towns will be kind
of, people will be in bed at midnight or at least
they'll be at home.

Some respondents distinguished between pubs and clubs in terms of the question of extended licenses. More thought pubs and bars should be granted extensions, while less thought that clubs should be open longer. Generally it was felt that pubs should be able to compete and provide an alternative to clubs, which were sometimes seen as overly expensive in terms of both entry fees and drinks. Extended licenses for live music venues and cafes were also heavily supported. While some club-goers thought that 2:00 am was generally sufficient in terms of providing alcohol, a number of respondents felt that dancing could be extended (say till 4), or that managers themselves should have the power to stay open as long as they wished.

Of the remaining 23% of the sample who suggested that the licensing laws should stay the same, the main reasons given were that there was ample amount of drinking time and that extending hours would indeed create more social problems. Although there appears to be little evidence to support this assertion it is interesting to note that a number of Scottish and European cities have recently cut back on extended licences for various reasons. A video produced in conjunction with the Institute of Popular Culture at Manchester

Metropolitan University however, suggests that many of the problems associated with the night-time economy in Britain are in fact due to the phenomenon of 'kicking out' punters at the customary 11:15 watershed, thereby creating potential trouble around queues for food and transport. While the available evidence appears to be somewhat contrary, it is clear that young adults overwhelmingly support the idea of extended hours. It would seem that there is a strong argument for experimentation with licenses, with the proviso that close monitoring might help to settle some of these arguments. The debate however should not be limited to a simple time/ consumption equation, but raises broader issues around changing the culture of drinking and the role licensing might play in creating alternative places and styles of going out in cities.

Alternative nightlife provision

The notion of 'alternative' provision arose from our analysis of material collected on young adults' dissatisfaction with various aspects of Newcastle nightlife, as well as what they felt the city was lacking. It also hinges on some of the broader changes and differentiation in young people's cultural identities mentioned earlier. The implications of developing alternative type of venues in the night time economy are far reaching and will affect not only opportunities to use this space, but influence modes of behaviour and change the image of city centres.

It is worth noting that the same percentage of the sample said the worst aspect of going out in Newcastle was the lack of alternative places, as those who mentioned violence as a problem. Furthermore, 43% of our respondents said the city was lacking either alternative clubs, areas, cafes or music venues. While the concept of alternative is used somewhat vaguely by different individuals in the sample, perhaps the best way to express the concept is to quote from one of them. What is interesting here is how this notion is usually linked to a particular place:

Geoff (L20)   *It is quite strange, I don't know what it is about the Wheatsheaf pub [name changed] and the Trinity House pub [name changed], but they do get a very strong clientele. I think it is the alternative scene, I think it is almost alternativeness, its not like there is any cohesiveness there. But you know the Trinity House is completely different to the Wheatsheaf, its soul music. You go to the Wheatsheaf and you have got a lot of alternative music as in indie and grunge. I think it is just the kind of atmosphere you're going to get in there, as I say it is relaxed. Z club [name changed] have got that underworld, you know, of basically people who smoke cannabis.*

Alternative refers generally to a casual, largely non-commercial, ecologically and ethnically influenced type of culture which privileges individual rights, style and identity. The idea of a 'counter-culture' in a collective sense is too strong considering the emphasis on diversity, individuality and personal taste, not to mention that the concept cuts across a range of more specific sub-cultural groups. As such, commentators have referred to different aspects of this general style as 'chaos culture' or 'permaculture' (The Crack, November 1992; The Guardian Weekend 8.1.94). Elements of 'post-rave, 'post-punk' and new ageism, like 'techno-hippies', 'dolies' (a politicised section of the young unemployed), squatters and anarchists ('hardcore') also fit into this catch-all category. Also, rather than being a 'minority', this non-mainstream amalgamation of groups is quickly becoming a significant section of the youth population.

It is this growing and somewhat ill-defined clientele which is fuelling the demand for alternative night-time provision. While Newcastle is generally regarded favourably in terms of its variety of pubs, a number of respondents argued that there could be more 'casual' establishments catering for this amorphous youth culture. This group was most vocal about legalising cannabis and tended to go to pubs and clubs where smoking was permissable. However, it was with respect to the club scene that the notion of alternative was most likely to be raised. Again the Riverside, and perhaps to a lesser extent World Headquarters and Planet Earth, stick out as possible models for what many young people say is lacking elsewhere. A large music venue similar to the Brixton Academy, a young person's collective, similar to Bradford's 1 in 12, and all nighter clubs were also mentioned.

One of the ideas often bandied about in terms of alternative provision is the notion of a more European cafe society or culture. For example, a study entitled 'Livable Towns and Cities' produced by the European Institute for Urban Affairs at Liverpool's John Moores University and commissioned by the Civic Trust, has argued that a city culture based on pedestrians, squares, concerts, restaurants and pavement cafes is essential for the revitalisation of urban space. The report states that the 'best antidote to fear of crime is the presence of people' and cites workable pilot projects in the US city of Chicago (The Guardian 16.12.93). Various other European and Scandinavian cities, like Rotterdam in Holland and Copenhagen in Denmark, have been held up as innovative examples of regenerated cities (Utne Reader September/ October, 1994; The Guardian 13.2.95).

Clearly Newcastle is poorly provided here, particularly in the evening. With minor exceptions, there are very few places outside of restaurants, which provide a cafe type atmosphere where one can choose between coffee, a snack or an alcoholic drink. The main place for coffee in the evening is most likely to be a multinational fast-food outlet. One of the immediate responses to this suggestion is that a European style approach would not work in this country, particularly in a city like Newcastle. One of the specific questions we asked our sample was whether they would use late night cafes which perhaps had a late license and served food. A resounding 83% of our respondents said that they would use such an establishment. Students in particular were very supportive of such a development, with 93% answering positively while 73% of locals also supported the idea. Interestingly, local women were also very keen on this type of provision, while local men appeared to be most adverse to the idea (still 60% said they would use such cafes).

Of those young adults who supported the idea of cafes, the main reasons appeared to revolve around a definite shift in many people's perceptions and views about night-time city culture. While they were viewed by some as a substitute for going out to noisy pubs and clubs, most saw cafes as an extension of their night out and were perceived as places where one could wind down, chill out or continue socialising. The idea of food and a hot drink were also appealing, as was being able to order an alcoholic drink, outside of a club, after 11 o'clock. There was also an expressed desire amongst a certain section of the young adult population for Dutch style cafes that permitted the smoking of cannabis. This view was defended by those who stated that this activity was condoned, if one was discreet, in a number of pubs and clubs in the city and that legalisation would remove the anxiety of possible criminal prosecution.

Of the 7% who said they would not use late night cafes, the majority being local men, the main reason given was that such a venue was not part of what they considered to be a proper night out. Hardcore clubbers also stated that cafes were probably a bit too quiet and they preferred extended licenses for nightclubs, while others suggested that these types of places might turn into trouble spots. Late night cafes in other major cities do not however have a history of disorder.[19]

The demand for alternative spaces in cities is not just limited to cafes, however popular they appear to be, but also includes thinking about providing different types of pubs, clubs and music venues as well as diverse restaurants and late-night cinema. This clearly ties in with the question of licensing hours, planning bylaws, urban policy and the development of city centre housing. The debate about alternative provision also raises wider issues about the role of the arts and popular culture in cities. Numerous European cities have identifiable 'youth areas', which consist of spaces for visual and performing arts, popular culture and shops and markets catering to various youth cultural styles. There are also broader questions about the expression of identity, the adoption of different lifestyles and inequality (i.e. the divided city). While the process of change will no doubt be a gradual one, young adult's existing cultures and desires might provide a basis for future experimentation and innovation here (Willis, 1990).

Widening access

In an earlier section on the divided city, it was suggested that it would be important to return to the question of policy-making in terms of widening access. While this encompasses broader issues and questions concerning equal opportunities and inequality generally, it also incorporates ideas concerning licensing and alternative provision discussed previously.

In a fundamental way, and despite the effects of post-industrialism and globalisation, Newcastle remains a working class city. In terms of nightlife it continues to meet the needs of its local population and this is displayed in its popularity and the high numbers of young people it attracts. The transformation of the night time economy in the city over the last fifteen years has not appeared to deter young adults from using it despite increased economic hardship and decline. If anything, one of the paradoxical effects of economic restructuring has been to increase the age range of locals using the city centre on nights out.

However, it is equally obvious that there is a 'breaking point' regarding the sacrifices and means by which young adults can continue to afford to use the city. Ironically, young working class people's apprenticeship to nights out in the town is located in some of the most expensive establishments in terms of drink prices, while many middle-class students take advantage of mid-week and union deals. There was some evidence in this research which shows that certain sections of the youth population, particularly those at home unable to claim any form of income, are becoming restricted from participating in this form of urban culture. The net effect of this social polarisation produces a kind of 'fortress mentality'- a stay away unless you can pay philosophy- and can have a negative impact on the further marginalisation of declining communities.

This is why future developments in the night time economy cannot be based on either economic or cultural exclusion. While the 'gentrification' of night time provision may encourage these social divisions, one should not automatically assume that the local population is unsupportive of diversity and change. As many young Geordies as students called for alternative venues and developments in the city centre and many more were branching out in terms of the variety and location of their nights out. The key point is that new and different does not necessarily have to mean exclusive and ultra-expensive. Yet, it is difficult to imagine how a repeat of the private sector's late 70s 'first wave' redevelopment of city centre pubs and clubs could be sustained in the 1990s without a heavy loss of custom or social exclusion.

There is also a close connection here between money, access and gender. Young local women are the social group most likely to be affected by further economic decline in the region or city centre nightlife becoming even more expensive. As has been shown, they already make dramatic sacrifices with respect to the percentage of their income spent on nights out, not to mention their higher levels of responsibility in the domestic household. Equal to these economic factors, young women also face the additional problem of safety and sexual harassment in the city centre. The extent of this phenomenon raises important questions about policing, club and pub management policies and issues about all-female transport. If the position of women in relation to the city is to continue to improve, these issues must be seriously addressed.

Racial discrimination and the ghettoisation of gay space regarding the night time economy also need to be tackled. While racism cannot be divorced from other issues like locality, housing policy and class culture, further research on the experiences of black and Chinese youth in the city is required. Careful monitoring of racial incidents in the city centre would also assist the need for more information. The debate about the 'Pink Triangle', the main gay area in the city, is not whether it should exist, but how it will develop in relation to the needs of the gay, lesbian and bi-sexual population and the attitudes of the wider heterosexual culture. In Manchester, for example, the city council has taken a more leading role in developing and even promoting the Gay Village as representative of a more cosmopolitan urban culture. While this does not automatically solve all the problems surrounding the politics of gay space, or tackle homophobia within the heterosexual community, it at least allows these debates to be raised.

Finally, it is important to return once more to the issue of student-local relations. Conflict and division between these groups were apparent with respect to their use of the city and much work needs to be done on breaking down stereotypes and building up links between the two communities. Students are also very much at the forefront of the local dance and music scene and were active in calling for alternative types of night-time venues and activities. They were the biggest supporters of the development of a cafe culture in the city, involving the granting of extended licenses. With regard to going out, students deserve to be heard not just as potential customers, but as active participants and contributors to the future of the night time economy.

The role of the city council

In the introduction to this book it was mentioned that one source of criticism concerning the research came from local politicians. In essence while their main critique focused mainly on the financial element, there was also an implicit assumption that the phenomenon of going out was of little interest to them in terms of policy-making outside of a social problem perspective. This rather contradictory vacillation between a 'moral panic' and a 'hands off' approach by local council leaders negates their underlying responsibility for controlling and intervening into many aspects of the night-time economy and urban policy.

We asked our sample of young adults whether or not they felt that Newcastle city council could do anything to improve the quality of their night out and nearly 60% answered in the affirmative. There were really three main issues raised- transportation, alternative provision of night-time facilities and safety.

Transport was by far and away the most frequent response made by our sample when asked about the city council's role in relation to nights out. While the majority appeared to be relatively happy with the quality of transportation, comments ranged from problems with existing services, as well as touched on wider issues surrounding future transport policy in the city. For instance, there was a general call for an improvement in the number of trains and buses running around the 'peak' closing time (i.e. 11:15-11:45). Others requested an extension of late night services in conjunction with a change of licensing hours and to cover clubs. Thirteen percent of women in our sample also suggested that the council had a role to play in providing female only buses and encouraging more female taxi companies/ women taxi drivers.

The second item concerned the council's position on licensing and the provision of alternative night-time facilities. In terms of the first point, it was recognised that they played an important role in the licensing debate, in terms of influencing local magistrates to grant not only more licenses but extensions to existing premises. For example, although the existing club scene in Newcastle was seen to be improving, it was felt that the council might have a role to play in helping this sector to expand through allowing more places to spring up and stay open longer. Alternative provision like late night cafes and special all night venues were also mentioned. Finally, it was felt that the city council had a financial role to play in considering the need for a youth centre or cooperative and a high quality purpose built music venue in the city centre.

Finally, our sample mentioned the issue of safety in relation to the activities of the city council. Previously we reported on young adult's overall satisfaction with the policing of the city centre and general support for the use of the CCTV cameras. However, there were additional requests for more bus and Metro conductors to help reduce the risk of violence on those services and at the end of the journey home. Complaints about poor lighting and dark passage ways in the city centre were mentioned by many young women as a safety issue, as was the request for all female buses and women taxi drivers.

In comparison to many other English, Scottish and Irish city councils, Newcastle appears to be more in the tradition which has tried to control and stultify the night-time economy (Lovatt, 1994). A number of young adults in our sample berated them for their lack of vision and failure to see the opportunities and benefits such an expansion might have for the city. Clearly such a policy would require some careful thought and planning, as well as some kind of financial commitment. The development of the Temple Bar area of Dublin and current discussions surrounding the Oldham Street area of Manchester are two possible models where youth culture has been used as a positive force.[20] The irony is that Newcastle city centre in the evening is currently viewed as a problem area to be contained, rather than as a potential opportunity for growth, creativity and alternative development.

Whereas creativity [in cities] this century and last was about hard infrastructures- sewers, electricity, transport- the creativity of the coming century will be about 'soft' infrastructures- creating a safe environment, encouraging networks of voluntary organisations, a lively after-dark economy...(Landry and Bianchini, 1995)

7. Conclusions

Rather than viewing going out as purely a frivolous pastime, this book has argued that it has become a more central element in the construction of young adult's identities, and this has important implications for how cities are and should be used.

The key finding is that the social significance and meaning of nights out has been transformed from a simple rite of passage to a more permanent socialising ritual for young adults. Two of the main processes underlying this shift of emphasis are economic restructuring and young people's experience of modern life through cultural consumption in the city. The creation and institutionalisation of a 'post-adolescent' phase has resulted in both the reformation of local, social and personal identities and a differentiation of youth cultures in the contemporary period.

The existence and significance of youth cultural identification in the post-industrial city extends far beyond either the realm of the trivial or a social problem perspective- two approaches which have often framed this phenomenon. At the broadest level, the issue raised is nothing less than a microcosm of deciding what type of society we want and what kind of citizens we want to live in it. The future of regional identities, particularly for young people, in the context of global economic capitalism and the sharpening of the cultural consequences of modernity, are also key elements in this debate. More specific concerns about changing households and family forms, the future of work and community organisation, not to mention more contemporary issues like citizenship and social polarisation, consumption and identity politics, also are represented here. Finally, urban youth cultures are a way into a debate about the future of post-industrial cities, and raise questions about what we want them to be like, how should they be used, and by whom?

It is at this last level that I want to pitch my concluding remarks, even though this concern is representative of these wider social, cultural and economic debates. Young people often are used as a barometer for assessing the society we all live in. The very fact that most discussions surrounding youth in the city have adopted a 'moral panic' type of approach should alert us to the fact that some of the creative possibilities may be missed and real problems hidden from view. The obsessional focus on drinking, promiscuity and violence with respect to nights out for instance, obscures many of the positive features of certain youth cultural forms. This is not to argue that these former points are unimportant. However, the way in which they are raised and discussed, often excludes the views of young adults themselves, or are based on unsubstantiated information.

This research has attempted to address many of these issues and put them into some kind of social context. It has also sought to utilise the voices of young adults themselves in defining some of the main problems facing the post-industrial city. For instance, it is clear that the future vibrancy of Newcastle nightlife hinges on not only the success of a wider regional economic strategy, but one that encourages urban development which does not exclude those already living in marginalised communities. Issues like sexual harassment, local-student conflict, racism and homophobia, all point towards policies necessary to widen and increase access to the city centre for women, black people, gays, lesbians, bisexuals and students. Finally, according to young adults themselves, various nightlife services could be improved and issues like over-regulation, in terms of licensing, and alternative provision need to be addressed.

The city council has a key role to play here in terms of its wider economic strategy, planning and housing policy in the city centre, licensing and the provision of various services. This is not to suggest that urban development and the revitalisation of cities is, or even should be, the sole responsibility of local government. Councils throughout the country have come under increasing political and financial pressure from central government and many, including Newcastle, are having difficulty maintaining even essential services. While local authorities are one of the main providers of what Landry and Bianchini (1995) refer to as 'hard infrastructure', and should continue to be, they have, as elected representatives, another important role to play in coordinating the debate about the future of the post-industrial city. Part of this means listening to some of the muted voices from below and building on the 'soft infrastructures'

110

created through the cultures of young adults in the city. While it would be foolish to suggest that a policy of expanding the night-time economy would solve all of the regions problems, there is clearly ample amounts of 'energy' there to fuel at least some of the future 'coals of Newcastle'.

Notes

1. For example see McRobbie (1984), Brake (1985), Hollands (1990),
    Willis (1990), Evans (1990), Worpole (1992), Henderson (1993),
    Redhead (1993) and Evans, Fraser and Taylor (1993).

2. While the research was initially conceived within broad academic and
    policy oriented parameters, it has also been heavily influenced by
    responses by the local culture, not to mention media and public
    reaction generally. For example, before even commencing the
    research was reported in both local papers (including subsequent
    coverage in letters/ features), two local radio broadcasts, both local
    TV news programmes (BBC and ITV), Radio 5, BBC Northern
    Ireland, a Canadian radio programme called 'As It Happens' (CBC
    Radio) and eight national dailies. Coverage also found its way into
    the 'Egyptian Gazette', 'Der Spegiel' (a German paper), and a Hong
    Kong newspaper. Requests were later made by the German and
    Japanese print media to develop the story. The principal investigator
    was also approached by Women's Hour, the Channel 4 TV
    programme 'The Word', the Today programme, ITN national news
    and three TV companies wanting to develop the research subject into
    a documentary programme, all of which were subsequently turned
    down. Media coverage of the project raises important questions about
    how sociological research is understood by the public outside
    academia.

3. For example, we sought to match our sample with a range of data
    derived from the 1991 Tyne and Wear Census for the 16-29 year old
    age group including economic activity, percentage unemployment and
    in education, social class, ethnicity, and marital status (see Table
    One and Two for examples of this).

4. One of the significant features of the decline of manufacturing and
    the rise of the service sector has been a gradual rise in the number
    of women in employment in Tyneside. Women, as a percentage of
    those employed in the local labour market, rose from 31% in 1961 to
    44.8% in 1984 (Robinson, 1988). The 1991 Census showed that in
    Tyne and Wear the percentage of women employed had risen by
    3.2% while it had fallen by 5.5% for men since 1981. Recent
    commentary on gender roles (Wilkinson, 1994) suggests that
    economic and social change has begun to completely transform the
    identities of women in the 18-34 year old category. However,
    numerous studies have also shown that women's employment in the
    region is located primarily in service industries and that much of it is

part-time and low paid (Robinson, 1988; Stubbs and Wheelock, 1992). Local evidence also suggests that women are still being expected to shoulder the main burden of domestic labour, despite their move into employment, even if their male partner is unemployed (Wheelock, 1990). Yet our research reveals some fundamental changes in young women's position in relation to the night-time economy, despite their still weak economic position.

5. All of the names of our respondents have been changed in the book. The name is followed by either a L for local or S for student and then the persons age (i.e. Sue (L19)- a 19 year old local women). RH refers to Robert Hollands the principal investigator and RT is Rosalind Taylor the project's research assistant. We indicate when the names of pubs and clubs have been changed (i.e. to protect the identity of an establishment), otherwise we have left them as is.

6. The notion of a post-modern youth culture, while remaining a complex academic perspective, has been taken up in both the cultural industries (i.e. music journalists, TV producers, promoters, the media) and by commercial market research and forecasting agencies. The basic scenario is one which emphasizes a communication-based global culture which is highly fragmented in terms of style and social values. Social class in particular is dismissed as largely irrelevant and outdated here (other social relations appear to be diminishing as well), while youth consumption and fashion becomes a 'pick and mix' affair. Youth identities in post-modernism and post-capitalism are reduced to the adage, 'you are what you wear'.
While there is clearly some food for thought here, post-modern theories are, in our view, currently inadequate for understanding either youth generally or providing an adequate theoretical basis for the analysis of youth cultures in the city. Despite rapid change, young people are still located within families, communities and regions and are still connected to the adult world through education, work and even the media. Additionally, we would want to argue that economic factors and social relations like class, gender and race continue to be important markers and provide a social context for youth cultural divisions. These include not only examples of exclusion and inequality amongst the youth population (including sexism and racism), but also help to explain a convergence of styles and values across the classes. Similarly, while the emphasis on globalisation and communication is a useful one, post-modernist approaches appear to give little weight to the importance of locality and local appropriations of global culture.

113

7.   A weekend newspaper article, covering the death of Viv Graham, a
     notable Newcastle 'hard man' who made a living out of his physical
     prowess, first as a bouncer and then as an 'enforcer' who was paid
     protection money to keep a number of pubs and clubs orderly in the
     city, appeared to suggest that this line of work was becoming an
     'alternative career' in the area. The assertion was that Tyneside gyms
     had never been so full of young men pumping iron (The Independent
     13.3.94). Additionally, research conducted by the principal researcher
     (Young and Hollands, 1994) into drug use and 'harm reduction' policy
     in the North has revealed that steroid rather than heroin users are the
     main beneficiaries of some needle exchange programmes in the
     region. The expression of masculinity in leisure, sport (including
     football supporters), criminality and as an 'alternative' employment
     career, in the context of the decline of manual/ physical work,
     deserves additional study.

8.   This calculation includes subtracting 20% of the total number of visits
     to account for periods of time where the sample might not have been
     able to go out consistently (i.e. lack of money, holidays, accident etc).

9.   For example see Lee (1987) for a discussion of the Chicago School
     approach, Castells (1983) for a Marxist perspective and McKenzie
     (1989) for a feminist analysis. One of the difficulties in utilising such
     a concept like the divided city however concerns not only which
     social groupings are divided, but where, why and by what processes.
     Another problem lies with the fact that such divisions often blur
     important distinctions and differences within a given population and
     may work to stereotype a social grouping. And finally, underlying all
     this is the normative issue concerning whether one interprets such
     divisions as either positive or negative. While we will present some
     evidence to suggest that Newcastle indeed is a divided city in terms
     of its nightlife, it will be important keep all these points in mind and
     view the issue as a complex one.

10. This is not the same argument Charles Murray (1990) uses to
     advance the idea that Britain has an emerging underclass.
     Campbell's (1993) work in fact is highly critical of Murray's position
     and looks instead at how patriarchy and economic restructuring
     combine to create marginal communities and antagonistic gender
     relations. Additionally this research found no evidence to support
     Murray's dubious notion of an underclass.

11. While many of these risk behaviours are largely symbolic, a small minority could be seen as potentially dangerous and or anti-social. Two in particular requiring further study might be risk cultures associated with sexuality (i.e. unprotected sex) and another associated with the thrill of physical violence.

12. These calculations include alcohol consumption in local pubs as well as the city centre (but not drinking at home), in order to make them more comparative with the figures from Regional Trends.

13. This comment is not intended to play down the seriousness of cases like Adam Brown, who was brutally beaten to death in the city centre in January 1995 or the senseless stabbing of Brian Anderson in the Bigg market later in the year.

14. While recognising that such data might be effected by a certain degree of 'subjectivity', fear of labelling or retribution, and an inability to remember past events clearly, we would argue that it is extremely valuable in two ways. First, this kind of data collection is reminiscent of 'victim' surveys carried out in relation to the experience of crime (i.e. the British Crime Survey), rape and sexual harassment, and these surveys are often used as a measure of the 'true' extent of these incidents (when compared with either public perceptions, media-based or 'official' accounts). While we were asking the sample to remember over a substantially longer period of time, we were surprised at the certainty and level of detail people had when discussing these events. Most certainly had clear recollections of their own personal involvement in incidents of violence. Second, this information also provides us with an important sense of young adults' perceptions and attitudes towards violent behaviour.

15. While there is a long tradition of sub-cultural analysis of youth in America (Albert Cohen and Walter Miller amongst others- see Brake, 1985), the most well recognised British tradition is that pioneered by the Centre for Contemporary Cultural Studies (CCCS) at the University of Birmingham (Hall and Jefferson, 1976). For a different variation of this perspective also see Hebdige (1979). While there are a number of weaknesses with this sub-cultural perspective, we would argue that any contemporary approach to youth culture needs to at least take on board the theoretical basis of this approach, particularly the class element, in order to advance a more comprehensive analysis. A reworked update of a cultural position can be found in Willis (1990), and to a more limited extent in Hollands (1990), ch 7.

16.   More recently, a local businessman whose plans to convert an old bar at Newcastle Central Station were turn down, argued against the magistrates charge that granting a license would cause more public disorder by stating that the pub 'is away from the Bigg Market and will attract families rather than lager louts' (Newcastle Herald and Post, October 19, 1995).

17.   This particular event attracted some 1200 people, while at the same time Northumbria police were trying to close down a rave club elsewhere in the city which was attracting less than 100 customers.

18.   One recent journalistic article has defined 'new age' as: 'The loose term that has emerged to cover all kinds of "alternative" behaviour-encompasses travellers, crusties, techno-crusties, convoy people, tribes and posses, all joined together by their liking for black leggings and green politics, their contempt for "the state" and often vaguely expressed desire for freedom'. Jo-Ann Goodwin 'A dark age', The Guardian Weekend (May 7, 1994).

19.   While Bewley's in Dublin is not licensed to sell alcohol, it is a model example of a place where one can enter, unimpeded by a burly doorman, and sit down and have bacon and eggs or a croissant in peace at 2:30 am after a night out on the town.

20.   I am indebted to John Dunne of the National Youth Bureau in Dublin and Justin O'Conner from the Institute of Popular Culture, Manchester Metropolitan University for drawing my attention to and showing me around these two areas.

References

Allatt, P. and Yeandle, S. (1992) *Youth Unemployment and the Family*, London, Routledge.

Aggleton, P. (1987) *Rebels Without a Cause*, London, Falmer.

Aggleton, P. (1990) *Health*, London, Tavistock.

Bagguley, P. et al (1990) *Restructuring: Place, Class and Gender*, London, Sage.

Banks, M. et al (eds) (1992) *Careers and Identities*, Milton Keynes, Open University Press.

Beck, U. (1992) *Risk Society: Towards a New Modernity*, London, Sage.

Bell, D. (1994) 'Bi-sexuality- A Place on the Margins', in Whittle, S. (ed), *The Margins of the City: Gay Men's Urban Lives*, Aldershot, Arena.

Blackie, J. (1993) 'Women's Leisure Experiences and Their Use of Public Leisure Provision in Newcastle Upon Tyne', unpublished MA dissertation, Leeds Metropolitan University.

Bonnett, A. (1993) *Radicalism, Anti-racism and Representation*, London, Routledge.

Brake, M. (1985) *Comparative Youth Cultures*, London, Routledge.

Bryman, A. and Cramer, D. (1994) *Quantitative Data Analysis for Social Scientists*, London, Routledge.

Campbell, B. (1993) *Goliath: Britain's Dangerous Places*, London, Methuen.

Castells, M. (1983) *The City and the Grassroots*, London, Arnold.

Centre for Research on Crime, Policing and the Community (CRCPC) (1993), *Evaluation of the Urban Crime Fund*, Report to Northumbria Police, CRCPC, University of Newcastle.

Charlton, R.J. (1894) *A History of Newcastle Upon Tyne from the Earliest Records to its Formation as a City.*

Coffield F. and Gofton, L. (1994) *Drugs and Young People*, London, Institute for Public Policy Research.

Colls, R. and Lancaster, B. (1992) *Geordies: The Roots of Regionalism,* Edinburgh, Edinburgh University Press.

Common, J. (1951) *Kidder's Luck*, London, Turnstile Press.

Dennis, N. and Erdos, G. (1992) *Families Without Fatherhood*, London, Institute for Economic Affairs.

Douglas, M. (ed) (1987) *Constructive Drinking*, Cambridge, Cambridge University Press.

Elms, R. (1988) 'Nightclubbing' *The Face*, No. 100.

Evan, K and Fraser, P. and Taylor, I. (1993) 'Going to Town: Routine Accommodations and Routine Anxieties in Respect of Public Space and Public Facilities in Two Cities in the North of England', a paper presented at the international Conference on the Public Sphere, Parker's Hotel, Manchester, January.

Evans, S (1990) 'Nightclubbing: An Exploration After Dark', Working Paper, University of Sheffield.

Featherstone, M. (1987) 'Lifestyle and Consumer Culture', *Theory, Culture and Society*, 4, 1.

Frith, S. (1978) *The Sociology of Rock*, London, Constable.

Giddens, A. (1990) *The Consequences of Modernity*, Cambridge, Polity.

118

Gofton, L. (1983) 'Real Ale and Real Men', *New Society*, November 17.

Gofton, L. (1986) 'Drink and the City', *New Society*, December 20/27.

Gofton, L. (1990) 'On the Town: Drink and the 'New Lawlessness'', *Youth and Policy*.

Griffin, C. (1985) *Typical Girls?*, London, Routledge.

Griffin, C. (1993) *Representations of Youth*, Cambridge, Polity.

Hall, S. and Jefferson, T. (eds) (1976) *Resistance Through Rituals*, London, Hutchinson.

Hammersley, M. (1992) *What's Wrong With Ethnography?*, London, Routledge.

Harvey, D. (1989) *The Condition of Postmodernity*, Oxford, Basil Blackwell.

Hebdige, D. (1979) *Subculture*, London, Methuen.

Henderson, S. (1993) 'Young Women, Sexuality and Recreational Drug Use', Manchester, Lifeline.

Hindle, P. (1994) 'Gay Communities and Gay Space in the City', in Whittle, S. (ed), *The Margins of the City: Gay Men's Urban Lives*, Aldershot, Arena.

Hollands, R. (1990) *The Long Transition: Class, Culture and Youth Training*, London, Macmillan.

Hollands, R. (1994) 'Back to the Future? Preparing Young Adults for the Post-Industrial Wearside Economy', in Garrahan P. and Stewart, P. (1994) *Urban Change and Renewal: The Paradox of Place*, Aldershot, Avebury.

Hope, T. (1983) *The Prevention of Disorder Associated With Licensed Premises*, Newcastle, Northumbria Police.

Lancaster, B. (1992) 'Newcastle- Capital of What?' in Colls, R. and Lancaster, B. (1992) *Geordies: The Roots of Regionalism,* Edinburgh, Edinburgh University Press.

Landry, C. and Bianchini, F. (1995) *The Creative City*, London, Demos in association with Comedia.

Lee, H. (1987) *Myths of the Chicago School*, Aldershot, Avebury.

Lewis, M. (1994) 'A Sociological Pub Crawl Around Gay Newcastle' in Whittle, S. (ed) (1994) *The Margins of the City: Gay Men's Urban Lives*, Aldershot, Arena.

Lovatt, A. (1994) 'Out of Order: Hyper-regulation in the City', a paper presented at the conference 'City Cultures, Lifestyles and Consumption Practices, University of Coimbra, Coimbra, Portugal, July 14-14, 1994.

MacDonald, R. (1994) 'Review of 'Rave Off'', *Youth and Policy*, 43.

MacDonald, R., Banks, S. and Hollands, R. (1993) 'Youth and Policy in the 1990s', *Youth and Policy*, 40 (Spring).

MacKinnon, K. (1989) 'Sexuality, Pornography and Method', *Ethics*, Vol 99, No. 2.

McCarthy, P. and Humphrey, R. (1994) 'Debt: The Reality of Student Life', *Higher Education Quarterly*, No 49, No 1, January.

McConville, B. (1983) *Women Under the Influence*, London, Virago Press.

McKenzie, S. (1989) 'Women in the City' in Peet, R. and Thrift, N. (eds), *New Models in geography*, London, Unwin Hyman.

McRobbie, A. (1984) 'Dance and Social Fantasy' in A. McRobbie and M. Nava (ed) *Gender and Generation* (Mamillan).

McRobbie (1993) 'Shut up and Dance: Youth Culture and Changing Modes of Femininity', *Cultural Studies*, 7, 3, October.

A. Marsh, J. Dobbs and A. White, *Adolescent Drinking* (London: HMSO, 1986).

Marsh, P. (1980) 'Violence at the Pub', *New Society*, June 12.

Merchant J. and MacDonald, R. (1994) 'Youth and the Rave Culture, Ecstasy and Health', *Youth and Policy*, No 45 (Summer).

Morrison, B. (1994) 'Brave New World on the Tyne', *The Independent on Sunday*, December 4.

Murray, C. (1990) *The Emerging British Underclass*, London, Institute for Economic Affairs.

Newcombe, R. (1991) *Raving and Dance Drugs*, Liverpool, Rave Research Bureau.

O'Conner, J. and Wynne, D. (n.d.) 'From the Margins to the Centre: Cultural Production and Consumption in the Post-Industrial City', *Working Papers in Popular Cultural Studies*, No.7, Manchester Institute for Popular Culture.

Redhead, S. (ed) (1993) *Rave Off: Politics and Deviance in Contemporary Youth Culture*, Aldershot, Avebury.

Robinson, F. (ed) (1988) *Post-Industrial Tyneside*, Newcastle, Newcastle City Libraries.

Robinson, F. (1994) 'Something Old, Something New? The Great North in the 1990s', in Garrahan P. and Stewart, P. (1994) *Urban Change and Renewal: The Paradox of Place*, Aldershot, Avebury.

Sande, A. (1994) 'The Use of Alcohol in the Ritual Process', unpublished paper, Norlands Research Institute, Bodo, Norway.

Savage, M. and Warde, A. (1993) *Urban Sociology, Capitalism and Modernity*, London, Macmillan.

Shields, R. (1991) *Places on the Margin: Alternative Geographies of Modernity*, London, Routledge.

Stubbs, C and Wheelock, J. *A Woman's Work in the Changing Local Economy*, Avebury, Aldershot, 1990.

Tuck, M. (1989) *Drinking and Disorder: A Study of Non-metropolitan Violence*, London, Home Office Research Study 108.

Tyneside Tec (1993) *Training People...Developing Business: Labour Market Report 1992-93*.

West, P. (1993) 'Youth Culture and Health Behaviour', a paper presented at the Centre for Health Services Research, University of Newcastle, December 14.

Wheelock, J. (1990) *Husbands at Home*, London, Routledge.

Whittle, S. (ed) (1994) *The Margins of the City: Gay Men's Urban Lives*, Aldershot, Arena.

Wilkinson, H. (1994) *No Turning Back: Generations and the Genderquake*, London, Demos.

Wilkinson, S. and Cornford, J. (1990) *The Popular Music Industry and Urban and Regional Development on Tyneside*, Centre for Urban and Regional Development Studies, University of Newcastle, October.

Willis, P. (1984) 'Youth Unemployment- A New Social State', *New Society*, 67.

Willis, P. (1990) *Common Culture*, Milton Keynes, Open University Press.

Wilson, E. (1991) *The Sphinx in the City*, London, Virago Press.

Wolfe, N. (1994) *Fire With Fire*, London, Chatto and Windus.

Worpole, K. (1992) *Towns for People: Transforming Urban Life*, Buckinghamshire, Open University Press.

Young C. and Hollands, R. (1994) 'How Far Has the Northern Region Adopted a Harm Reduction Approach to Dealing with Drug Misuse?', *Youth and Policy*, No. 45.